LIGHTHOUSES
of North America

LIGHTHOUSES
of North America

JACOB ATTWELL

METRO BOOKS
NEW YORK

METRO BOOKS
New York

An Imprint of Sterling Publishing Co., Inc.
1166 Avenue of the Americas
New York, NY 10036

ISBN 978-1-4351-6872-5

For information about custom editions, special sales, and premium and corporate purchases, please contact Sterling Special Sales at 800-805-5489 or specialsales@sterlingpublishing.com.

Manufactured in China

2 4 6 8 10 9 7 5 3 1

sterlingpublishing.com

CONTENTS

INTRODUCTION
6

Chapter One
LIGHTHOUSES OF THE GREAT LAKES
14

Chapter Two
LIGHTHOUSES OF THE NORTHEAST
50

Chapter Three
LIGHTHOUSES OF THE SOUTHEAST
106

Chapter Four
LIGHTHOUSES OF THE WEST
162

Chapter Five
LIGHTHOUSES OF CANADA
208

INDEX
254

ACKNOWLEDGEMENTS
256

INTRODUCTION

A lighthouse is a tower, building, or other structure designed to emit light from a system of lamps and lenses or, in older times, from fires, and used to aid navigation for pilots at sea on inland waterways.

Introduction

On rocky cliffs and sandy shores across all of North America, hundreds of colorful stone structures stand with pride overlooking the blue waters below, some still on watch with a bright beacon of light at the top. Others rest quietly in crumbles, their heyday far behind them. Either way, their presence is stoic and their history, unforgettable. They are the lighthouses of a different era, and they each have an incredible story to tell.

Before lighthouses became a part of the American and Canadian landscape, early maritime sailors used hillside fires to guide captain and crew back to shore. The orange blazes could be seen from miles away, helping large vessels navigate with ease on even the darkest of nights. But towns and villages lacking steep hillsides had to be more creative. In order for the bright fires to be seen from the water, villagers were compelled to build tall, rock structures that rose as high as the steepest hills. Atop these structures, they lit a fire. It was the mid 18th century when these accidental engineers created the precursor of what would soon be called the lighthouse.

LEFT: The Pharos of Alexandria is one of the Seven Wonders of the Ancient World. This is a computer-generated illustration based on ancient records discovered by Hermann Thiersch in 1909.

ABOVE: The Boston Light is situated on Little Brewster Island in Boston Harbor, Massachusetts. The original lighthouse was built in 1716, but was destroyed in the Revolutionary War. It was rebuilt in 1783.

The next generation of lighthouses would become more sophisticated, boasting secure stone towers that allowed access to the top from an interior iron staircase that spiraled upward. The anatomy of the lighthouse would see a new shift in the early 19th century, when orange fires were replaced with oil-burning lamps. Several lighthouses used a metal framed birdcage-like casing with polygonal glass sides to protect the lamp and keep the flames from blowing out. Lighthouse keepers, as they were called, were responsible for

maintaining the beacon. They were charged with several duties, not the least of which was risking their lives to save sailors in trouble in the choppy waters below.

Many tales that surround the history of the more renowned lighthouses include stories of strife and struggle. Dangerous waters and storms took the lives of many. In order to save money, vessel engineers built poorly constructed ships that couldn't handle rough waters or unforeseen collisions. The vessels tore apart easily and, if there was a fire on board, burned quickly. If a lighthouse keeper was witness to the danger, part of his job was to do what he could to bring survivors back to shore.

All the while, the federal government watched the evolution of the lighthouse from afar. In 1789, the building and maintenance of coastal lighthouses fell upon the United States Secretary of the Treasury, Alexander Hamilton, and was noted as one of the first acts of Congress that same year. By 1850, the official US Government Lighthouse Board was established.

The First Lighthouse

The first lighthouse in North America was built in September of 1716 and was constructed in the Province of Massachusetts, which is now Little Brewster Island. The Boston News Letter reported: "...at the Entrance of the Harbour of Boston, in order to prevent the loss of the Lives and Estates of His Majesty's Subjects, The said Light House has been built; and on Fryday last the fourteenth Currant the Light was kindled, which will be very useful for all Vessels going out and coming in to the Harbour of Boston."

Three years later in 1719, the lighthouse in the harbor would become the first to include the likes of a "fog signal." On unclear nights when the fog was thick, a burning fire could only do so much. To alert boats of the presence of other ships and vessels or rocky coastlines, a canon was put on site. This concept would eventually evolve into the fog horn. In some cases, a bell or steam whistle was used to alert incoming ships.

ABOVE: The Sandy Hook Light is situated about one and a half miles inland from the tip of Sandy Hook, New Jersey. It is the oldest operating lighthouse in the United States.

On the other side of the world, thousands of years earlier, Egypt is noted as having the first ever lighthouse in history. Built sometime between 280 and 247 BC, the Lighthouse of Alexandria stood some 350 feet tall. One of the Seven Wonders of the Ancient World, the massive structure survived three earthquakes before it was abandoned in 1323. Eventually, it crumbled and some of the stones were used to build a city. However, In 1994, archeologists discovered lighthouse remains on the floor of Alexandria's Eastern Harbor. It was an exciting find for historians.

Lighting the Way for Sailors

Towers were lit in different ways over the centuries. Some used bonfires, while others used candles. More advanced lighthouses throughout North America began incorporating whale oil lamps in the mid-1700s.

For the next one hundred years, worldly engineers would work on improving the way lighthouses were lit, including an American ship captain by the name of Winslow Lewis. Lewis created a lamp and light system that included reflectors and a circular wick to prevent excessive smoking. Some historians believe he fashioned the light system almost exactly the same as the Argand lamp, a highly successful oil lamp created by Frenchman Francois Pierre Ami

Argand. Because Lewis forged friendships with members of the US Government Lighthouse Board, he was able to persuade them to use his lamps over any other. By 1816, all of the lighthouses in America were using his Argand-like lamp.

While Lewis' lights proved efficient and burned bright, there still remained the issue of proper diffusion of light. To combat the issue, a member of the French Lighthouse Establishment stepped up to solve

BELOW: General George Meade was an engineer and commander during the American Civil War. He designed and built many lighthouses along the eastern seaboard of the United States.

BELOW RIGHT: Another Civil War Veteran was Colonel Orlando M. Poe, who was responsible for a number of beautiful lighthouses on the Great Lakes.

RIGHT: The development of the Fresnal lens in 1822 revolutionized lighthouse operation all over the world.

LEFT: The Makapuu Point Light on the island of Oahu has the largest lens of any lighthouse in the United States. It was automated in 1974.

ABOVE: Swedish industrialist Nils Gustaf Dalén invented an automatic lamp system. It quickly came into worldwide use for buoys and unmanned lighthouses.

the problem. In 1822, Augustin Jean Fresnel created a glass lamp shaped like a beehive. His design was intentional and was created to refract beams of light so that they would shine out into the night sky horizontally. Known as the Fresnel lens, the innovation was remarkable and changed the face of the entire lighthouse system.

Fresnel passed away in 1827, but the concept of his lens lived on. Recognizing the power of the light, the Stevenson family of Scotland examined Fresnel's invention and began to improve upon it. Interestingly, author Robert Louis Stevenson was a relative of the Scottish family and started his career as a lighthouse engineer. Thanks to the work of the Stevensons the updated Fresnel lens illuminated the waters of lighthouses across the globe by the 1850s.

The Lonely Lighthouse Keeper

Every single lighthouse that dotted the North American landscape in the early years was manned by strong, able-bodied men between the ages of 18–50. His occupation title was "lighthouse keeper," and he did everything from tending to the light to rewinding the clockwork mechanism of heavy chains and weights that rotated the lens. Keepers were on call 24-hours a day. Flannel, indigo colored uniforms were a must. Excessive alcohol intake was frowned upon. Men with large families were favored. The federal government, which was responsible for employing the hard-working lighthouse keepers, quickly recognized that keepers with wives and children came with free labor was part of the package.

Twice a year, the lighthouse keepers received much-needed goods like food, fuel, and cleaning supplies. Some deliveries included books to help occupy the mind of the lonely keepers. If they were married,

the women took up knitting and helped clean. The children also did chores, like whitewashing the tower or cleaning windows. In the early mornings, they joined their father to fish or hunt.

The more mechanical and maritime experience the keepers had, the better. Having the ability to fix broken chains and man a boat was a necessity. Being able to swim and fight strong currents was also a must. With poorly constructed vessels transporting massive amounts of raw material, danger was inevitable. Lighthouse keepers heard of stories where fellow keepers and sailors lost their lives during disastrous ship fires or crashes. A keeper was considered lucky if he never had to make his way out to choppy waters during such tragedies.

With a long list of duties and responsibilities, the life of a keeper was a hard one. Because some of the lighthouses were secluded, workers there lived isolated lives, having very little interaction with anyone. It was a hard calling, but hundreds of men accepted.

By the early 1900s things began to shift for lightkeepers.Technology brought with it ideas of automation and electricity, slowly removing the federal employees from their stations, one by one. Gas was now being used as fuel as well. By the 1920s, a large majority of US and Canadian lighthouses functioned without manpower.

Those that don't have either been left to crumble or belong to state parks and historical societies. There are a handful that have been converted to bed and breakfasts. Whatever state they are in now, we've captured the essence of the most notable and beautiful standing lighthouses left in North America.

The following pages will guide you on a colorful tour of where they are, when they were built, and how they came to be. They are the lighthouses of a different era, and they each have an incredible story to tell.

ABOVE: Fanny May Salter, a lighthouse keeper in the United States Coast Guard service, polishes the lens in the Turkey Point Light, Maryland in 1945.

LIGHTHOUSES OF THE GREAT LAKES

At one point in history, the Great Lakes supported approximately 350 lighthouses on both sides of the Canadian-American border. Collectively, the lakes are considered the largest freshwater body on the planet, forming what is known as "inland freshwater sea." Because of where the Great Lakes are located, the weather patterns are often more violent than those on the ocean, making the strong, structural towers a much-needed commodity.

HOW TO GET THERE

The Cedar Point Light is located in Lighthouse Point, a small peninsula near Sandusky. The lighthouse stands tall above a handful of lakeside cottages. Take US 6 west toward the amusement park and turn right onto Cedar Point Drive. Visitors can tour the lighthouse between 10am and 5pm during the week.

Address
1 Cedar Point Dr.
Sandusky, OH 44870

Cedar Point Light

Built: 1862
Style: House Style
Height: 38 feet (11.58m)

Lake Erie was known in the early days for its dark waters and excessive fog. Plenty a stormy night turned ships upside down, compromising the lives of several crewmen. After a group of concerned citizens petitioned Congress in 1837, $2,500 was allocated to place a beacon and tower on the shore. Another $3,000 was added to the budget the following year. The first Cedar Point light was finished in 1839. In 1862, construction of a second, larger lighthouse began, this one with a square tower. This is the lighthouse present on the site today.

The current light atop the six-room limestone tower in Sandusky, Ohio brought vessels safely to shore until 1909 when the light was removed. Federal officials continued to use the structure for different reasons, including a rescue boat station until it was decommissioned in 1975. It stood quietly on the shore with no certain future.

Cedar Point is best known for its massive amusement park, packed with fast roller coasters and other unique rides. To accommodate the influx of visitors, the park bought the northwest corner of the peninsula in 1987, so they could add more real estate. Here sat the abandoned lighthouse, crumbling, and waiting for its demise. Despite the lantern being gone and part of the tower on the ground in a pile, the beauty of the lighthouse still remained. Park officials chose to restore the structure and improve the area surrounding it to bring back the feel of a maritime New England town. The exterior of the lighthouse opened to visitors in 2001.

LEFT: Cedar Points duties were transferred to Marblehead Coast Guard Station in 1975, and the Cedar Point station was discontinued.

Chicago Harbor Light

Built: 1893
Style: Rubble Stone
Range: 24 miles (39km)
Height: 48 feet (15m)

Before the Chicago Harbor Light was built atop the northern breakwall in the harbor, a light tower was erected on land in 1832. While it was helpful to a degree, more land lights were needed along the pier to help sailors navigate their way around the stones that jutted into Lake Michigan. Wooden pier lights were placed there, illuminating the pier's entrance. The light system of both land tower and pier lights stayed in place until a new cast iron tower was erected in the same place in 1859. In 1893, to mark the beginning of the

LEFT & ABOVE: The cast-iron Chicago Harbor Light originally stood on land at the mouth of the Chicago River. In 1919, it was moved to the end of a breakwater, a mile out in Lake Michigan, where it could function more effectively.

HOW TO GET THERE

The Chicago Harbor Light still stands as an automated, on duty tower on a breakwall in Lake Michigan.The lighthouse cannot be accessed by the public, but it can be viewed from the Navy Pier in Downtown Chicago. Available cruises can bring you in for a closer look. Chicago's First Lady Cruises depart below Michigan Avenue near the riverwalk. Call 847-358-1330 for reservations.

Address
Navy Pier
600 E Grand Ave.
Chicago, IL 60611

World's Fair, the existing lighthouse was built at the mouth of the Chicago River, detached from the mainland. The stone structure was equipped with a Fresnel lens.

This light saw lots of changes over the years. In 1925, the fog signal was upgraded to an air diaphone. Electricity was also installed that year. In total, three different lighthouses have guarded the Chicago Harbor over the years. As commerce grew on the waters and the city exploded into a military outpost, continuous upgrades and changes on the tower were necessary.

Today, the lighthouse is an automated, active structure that functions under the guise of the United States Navy. The red light at the top flashes every five seconds. It is the only remaining lighthouse in all of Chicago. Iconic in its own right, the lighthouse sees hundreds of visitors each year.

Eagle Harbor Light

Built: 1871
Style: Octagonal Red Brick
Range: 29 miles (46km)
Height: 60 feet (18.28m)

The shoreline of Michigan runs 3,288 miles long, making Michigan the home of more lighthouses than any other state. It's unclear how many standing structures still remain, but it is clear that one of the more notable lighthouses is Eagle Harbor on Lake Superior. Before the current structure was built in 1871, an original one and a half story 5-room house was built with a short, wooden tower and iron lantern. As with most lighthouses, it experienced upgrades with the light system and was soon enhanced with a Fresnel lens. In 1930, electricity controlled the beacon. In 1980, it became fully automated.

One of the more compelling tales surrounding Eagle Harbor is that of a rescue crew in 1926 that spotted an ice-covered ship on it's way back to harbor. Having already saved 22 men from the Thomas

Maytham, the crew brought the men ashore and headed back out to the ice-covered ship. They would soon learn this ship was called the City of Bangor. They rescued another 29 men still onboard. The vessel was transporting 200 Chrysler cars that night, many of which were destroyed. However, if you visit the lighthouse, one of the surviving Chryslers that was part of the cargo is there on display.

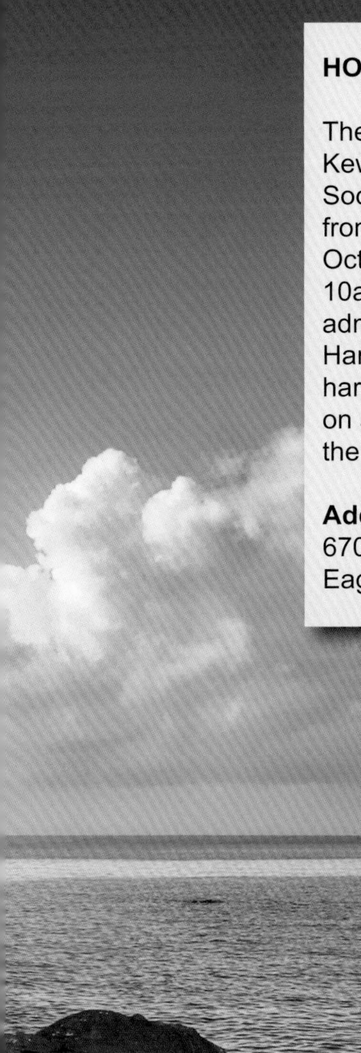

HOW TO GET THERE

The lighthouse is owned by the Keweenaw County Historical Society and is open to the public from the middle of June to early October. Hours of operation are 10am to 5pm. There is a small admission fee. Drive toward Eagle Harbor on west M-26. At the harbor and beach area, make a left on a small road that takes you to the parking area.

Address
670 Lighthouse Rd.
Eagle Harbor, MI 49950

LEFT & ABOVE: During the 1850s, the discovery of copper and iron ore in mountains, to the south and west, caused small ports, such as Eagle Harbor, to become established. The red-brick Eagle Harbor Light Station, built in 1851 and replaced in 1871, guards the rocky entrance to Eagle Harbor, guiding mariners across the northern edge of the Keweenaw Peninsula.

Fairpoint Harbor West Breakwater Light

Built: 1925
Style: Concrete Pierhead
Range: 13 miles (24km)
Height: 42 feet (13m)

This classic four-square structure in Fairport Harbor, Ohio was built in 1925 to replace the original Fairport Harbor Lighthouse that was constructed some 100 years earlier. In 1917, Congress passed a bill to fund the demolition of the first lighthouse, as well as the construction of the new one. However, local residents protested the demolition of the original and it was halted. Thanks to their efforts, tourists can visit the original structure that is now a popular maritime museum.

Today, the current lighthouse is one of the few in the US that has been transformed into a modern living space. Presently undergoing renovations, the structure includes a full kitchen, three bedrooms, and a family room. The property will soon be available as a vacation rental. Aside from this, the Fairport Harbor West Breakwater light will continue to serve as a navigational lighthouse maintained by the US Coast Guard.

"The lighthouse does great service to humanity; yet it is the slave of those who trim the lamps."

Alice Wellington Rollins

HOW TO GET THERE

The automated lighthouse is closed to the public, but can still be seen along the breakwater. Near the VIllage of Fairport Harbor about 30 miles east of Cleveland, the lighthouse is north of the village at the mouth of the Grand River. It can also be accessed through Headlands Beach State Park. To reach the park, take the OH-44 toward Headlands Road and turn right. The park will be on the left.

Address
Headlands Beach State Park
601 Headlands Rd.
Mentor, OH 44060

RIGHT: The Fairpoint Harbor West Breakwater Light is currently undergoing a refurbishment inside and out.

HOW TO GET THERE

To see the lighthouses and experience the pier, visit the boardwalk at Chinook Pier. The boardwalk is open from dawn to dusk. Take M-104 towards Spring Lake and Grand Haven. Turn left at the fork, follow the signs for US-31 S/Grand Haven, and then merge onto US-31 S/N to Beacon Boulevard. Turn right on Jackson Street. Jackson Street becomes North Harbor Avenue.

Address
Chinook Pier
301 North Harbor Ave.
Grand Haven, MI 49417

Grand Haven Pier Lights

South Pierhead Inner Light (large)
Built: 1905
Style: Conical Steel Tower
Height: 51 feet (15.5m)

Grand Haven Pier Light (small)
Built: 1858
Style: Wood, Steel on Concrete

Lights illuminating the Grand Haven River have been there since the first lighthouse site was established in 1839. Over the next sixty years, at least three different lighthouses, a fog signal house, and two cobblestone dwellings would be built to guide ships and ferries safely through the waters.

Today two red lighthouses connected by a well-lit catwalk don this location, bringing visitors from all over the world to view its beauty. The lantern room on the tallest tower, the South Pierhead Inner light, is still active and in use by the Coast Guard, blinking every four seconds. The lantern room here is encased in cast iron to protect the light from fierce Michigan storms and winters.

The Grand Haven Pier Light, the smaller of the two, has been moved further out into the pier at least twice between the years of 1870 and 1905. This was because as commerce and transportation grew, so did the need to improve the lighthouse structures and the lengthy pier that supported them. The concrete base of the smaller structure ensures the building is secure in the often choppy waters. A V-shaped design on the concrete portion faces the water and was added to the front of the smaller tower to "split" incoming waves to help protect it.

The lighthouses are not open for tours, but visitors can view them up close with a walk along the popular boardwalk at Chinook Pier on the Grand River channel.

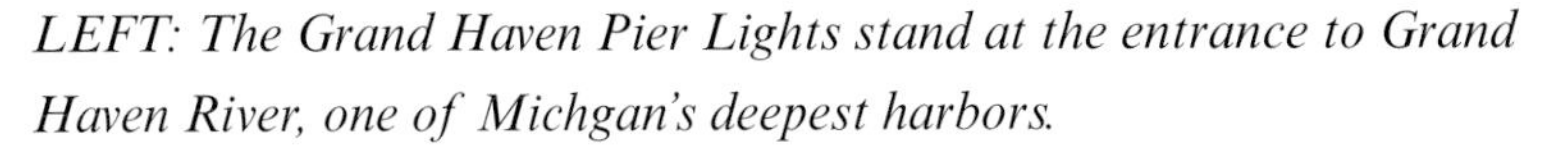

LEFT: The Grand Haven Pier Lights stand at the entrance to Grand Haven River, one of Michgan's deepest harbors.

Grand Traverse Light

Built: 1883
Style: House Style, Brick
Height: 39 feet (11.88m)

The Grand Traverse Lighthouse was built in 1883, illuminating the way for sailors in the Manitou Passage of Lake Michigan. Still active today at the tip of the Leelanau Peninsula, it boasts a working fog horn that once helped large vessels navigate rough waters. As is the case with most existing lighthouses, the structure on site isn't the original. The first lighthouse erected there in 1858 was 30 feet tall and had an unattached two-room house for the lighthouse keeper. The light at the top of the structure was made with six lamps and reflectors. In 1857, a Fresnel lens was installed.

In 1880 the site grew after a woodshed was added. Some ten years later, a two-story barn was constructed. The site was larger than most, and comfortably accommodated a keeper and his family. Despite all of the additions, the tower itself was considered "poorly built." It was torn down in 1883 and replaced with the current lighthouse. Built with Milwaukee cream city brick, the structure was given new life. Lighthouse keepers maintained the property until 1972.

Today it acts as a museum offering tours that commemorate the lives of the lighthouse keepers. The structure is tucked quietly inside of Leelanau State Park, offering historic tours, snowshoe walks, and more.

HOW TO GET THERE

This historic lighthouse is quietly tucked inside the Leelanau State Park, roughly nine miles north of Northport. Take M-22 toward Northport and exit to M-204. Follow the easy-to-spot "Lighthouse" signs as they guide you to Lighthouse Point Road. There is a small admissions fee. The lighthouse can be visited May through October and weekends in November.

Address
Leelanau State Park
15550 North Lighthouse Point Rd.
Northport, MI 49670

RIGHT: Grand Traverse Light is located at the tip of the Leelanau Peninsula, which separates Lake Michigan and Grand Traverse Bay.

Grosse Point Light

Built: 1873
Style: Tudor Revival
Height: 113 feet (34.44m)

Shipping disasters were plentiful in unguarded waters. One of note occurred in 1860, when the *Lady Elgin* ran into the *Augusta*, a ship transporting lumber. In less than an hour, the splintered Lady Elgin sunk below the waters. The following morning, dozens of Northwestern University students stood on shore searching the water for signs of life. One student, Edward W. Spencer, rescued 17 people that morning before he collapsed from exhaustion. Three hundred lives were lost that night, making the shipwreck of *Lady Elgin* one of the largest disasters of that time.

After this tragedy, Evanston residents lobbied the federal government for a lighthouse. Their voices were heard. Construction on the tall and mighty lighthouse was completed in 1873. But it took a bit longer for the completion of the lantern. It wasn't until March of 1874 that a Fresnel lens was installed and activated on the Grosse Pointe lighthouse. This powerful illumination could be seen 21 miles over the water on clearer nights.

In 1880, two fog signal buildings were erected on the site. By 1923, the tower was electrified. It was automated in 1935 and became decommissioned by the Coast Guard in 1941. The lighthouse today is a national landmark and museum. A hundred and forty-one stairs take curious visitors to the top where guided tours tell stories of maritime men and the lighthouse keepers that guided them to shore.

LEFT & RIGHT: The historic and beautiful Grosse Point Light is situated in a quiet Chicago suburb. Its 113-foot tower focuses a flashing beacon that is visible for many miles out in Lake Michigan.

HOW TO GET THERE

The lighthouse is located in the city of Evanston. From Interstate 94, take the Old Orchard exit and then turn right onto Old Orchard Road. Make a slight left onto Grosse Point Road. After a short distance, turn right onto Central Street. Go 2.6 miles and make a left on Sheridan Road. Parking can be found in the beach lot on the other side of the lighthouse. Tours are conducted June through September on weekends between 2pm and 4pm.

Address
2601 Sheridan Rd.
Evanston, IL 60201

Holland Harbor Light

Built: 1872
Style: Pierhead Beacon, Square Tower
Height: 45 feet (13.71m)

Early settlers understood the importance of waterway passages that allowed large ships and vessels to make their way through. However, in the small hamlet of Holland, Michigan there wasn't one. Therefore, townsfolk came together and dug a channel themselves, opening up the waterway between Black Lake and Lake Michigan in 1859. The first vessel to float through was a steamboat called *Huron*. As more boats and ships made their way through, it was clear that a lighthouse needed to be erected.

In 1872 the pierhead beacon lighthouse was built. Since then, the maritime station has seen its share of transformation. In 1907 a fog horn building was constructed on the site to ward of complaints that the lighthouse alone wasn't enough. In 1950 it was painted bright red after a pronouncement stated that any lighthouse on the right side of the harbor needed to be red. Today the structure is known to area residents as "Big Red."

Like many lighthouses, it nearly met its demise and threatened to be torn down in the mid-1970s. But residents fought back, passing around petitions in an effort to save the landmark. Their efforts paid off, and, 1974, the Holland Harbor Lighthouse Historical Commission was created.

BELOW & RIGHT: Nicknamed "Big Red," the Holland Harbor Light, like many of the lights along the eastern shore of Lake Michigan, is located at the end of a pier. In 1970, the Coast Guard recommended that the lighthouse be abandoned, but citizens circulated petitions to rescue it. The Holland Harbor Lighthouse Historical Commission was organized to preserve this historic landmark.

HOW TO GET THERE

From Downtown Holland, head north on River Avenue. Drive over the bridge and turn left onto Douglas Avenue. This will turn into Ottawa Beach Road. If you're coming from US-31, head west onto Lakewood Boulevard. This will eventually turn into Douglas Avenue and then Ottawa Beach Road.

Address
2215 Ottawa Beach Rd.
Holland, MI 49423

Mantiowoc Breakwater Light

Built: 1918
Style: Steel Square, Concrete
Range: 13 miles (24km)
Height: 40 feet (11.19m)

The original Manitowoc Breakwater Light was approved by Congress for construction in 1837. After $5,000 was appropriated to build the light, land on which to erect it needed to be sought. The state of Michigan was charged with this task and purchased the land from the local Jones family. Thereafter, workers began to build the original brick tower with an unattached dwelling nearby.

A fog signal building was added in 1892 to assist with guiding steamers. To further improve the area and protect the harbor, a 400-foot breakwater was also constructed later in 1895. Twice, the lighthouse was moved to improve navigation. But these moves weakened the original structure, forcing the construction of a new one. In 1918 the present lighthouse was erected with two galleries mounted on a steel square keeper's quarters.

Over the years the historic structure has fallen prey to graffiti and other damage. With the hopes of reviving it, Philip Carlucci of Melville, New York bought the lighthouse for $30,000. Carlucci's intention is to invest further to restore the landmark fully, eventually opening it up to the public for full view.

RIGHT & INSET: The harbor towns along the shores of Lake Michigan are proud of their lighthouses. In the coming years Manitowoc will be restored to its former glory by New York business man Philip Carlucci.

HOW TO GET THERE

Located on the north breakwater at the entrance of Manitowoc Harbor, the lighthouse is not yet open to the public. However, it can be viewed from a nearby walkway just past the Wisconsin Maritime Museum. To get there, enter downtown Manitowoc and take 1-43 to exit 149. Turn on Hwy 151. Go over a bridge and turn right on Maritime Drive. The lighthouse is past the Maritime Museum along the breakwater.

Address
Wisconsin Maritime Museum
75 Maritime Drive
Manitowoc, WI 54220

Marblehead Light

Built: 1821
Style: Square Stucco
Range: 7 miles (13km)
Height: 105 feet (32m)

The infamous Marblehead Lighthouse sits quietly and full of character on the Marblehead Peninsula. Made of white stucco and surrounded by a quaint, white fence, this lighthouse is the oldest active structure still in its original form on the Great Lakes. Visitors can take seventy-seven steps to the top where a Fresnel lens was once mounted. The lens, installed at the tower in 1903, is on display at the Coast Guard station near the lighthouse.

This lighthouse holds a great nugget of history because this is where the first female lighthouse keeper on the Great Lakes manned a tower. Her name was Rachel Wolcott, and she took over as keeper after her husband passed away in 1832. She didn't man the tower long, however. She remarried a short time later and her second husband became keeper. Sixteen keepers in total cared for the lighthouse until 1943 when the US Coast Guard assumed full responsibility of it.

Once featured on a US postage stamp, Marblehead has been seen on envelopes around the world. The lighthouse has appeared on Ohio's license plates, too. Now a part of the Ohio State Parks system, the landmark can be toured with a scheduled appointment.

BELOW & RIGHT: The Marblehead Light is the oldest continuously operating lighthouse on the Great Lakes. It was originally called the Sandusky Bay Light, because it marked the entrance to Sandusky Bay and the eastern end of the south passage between the Bass Islands and the Ohio shore. Its name was changed to the Marblehead Light in 1870.

HOW TO GET THERE

Take I-90 west toward Toledo. Merge onto OH-2 west toward Sandusky, and then OH-269 toward Marblehead. Turn right onto East Harbor Road, and then left on Lighthouse Drive. The park grounds are open all year long. Tours should be scheduled, and typically start Memorial Day Weekend.

Address
110 Lighthouse Dr.
Marblehead, OH 43440

New Presque Isle Light

Built: 1870
Style: "Poe" Style, Conical
Height: 113 feet (34.44m)

When commercial traffic on Lake Huron began to increase in the late 1800s, the government recognized the importance of erecting a coastal lighthouse at the north end of the Presque Isle Peninsula. It was the first "Poe" lighthouse built in the area, and the only one on Lake Huron. The light was designed by Brigadier General Orlando Metcalfe Poe, who would go on to design at least seven similar lighthouses in the Great Lakes. His style is recognized by the iron brackets on the catwalks that surround the lantern room, as well as the four stylistic windows featured below the catwalk.

The keeper's eight-room house was built on site in 1905, some 100 feet south of the tower. A short time later, two different fires, one in 1908 and another in 1911, threatened to take the lives of the keepers there. The latter fire was so intense, surrounding trees needed to be cut down to create a firewall as firemen battled the blaze with water hoses. Repairs were made and life continued for the keepers.

Today, A gift shop and museum displays are located here next to the tower. Here, the original Fresnel lens can be viewed. The lens was removed from the tower in 2003 and tucked away in storage until it was brought back out for the public to view in 2012. The new Presque Isle light is the tallest on the Great Lakes, with 138 iron steps to the top. When skies are clear, visitors can see across Lake Huron to Great Duck Island.

LEFT & RIGHT: The Old Presque Isle Light (left) was built to warn Lake Huron shipping of the need to turn north-west towards the safe passage that led to the Sraits of Mackinac and Lake Michigan. Its beacon was not quite powerful enough for the task, however, and President Lincoln ordered a taller tower to be built, that was completed in 1871. This is known as the New Presque Isle Light (see right).

HOW TO GET THERE

From the Alpena Regional Medical Center on Chisholm Street, drive 8.7 miles to East Grand Lake Road and turn right. Follow the road to the stop sign where you'll turn right to stay on East Grand Lake Road. The new lighthouse is about ten miles down.

Address
4500 E Grand Lake Rd.
Presque Isle, MI 49777

HOW TO GET THERE

Visitors will take 1-75 into Mackinaw City and exit off of 336 onto Nicolet Avenue. From there, make a right onto Huron Avenue. The parking lot for the lighthouse is just two blocks down from the turn. There are picnic tables for lunching in the area. Tours are available May through October for an admission fee.

Address
526 North Huron Ave.
Mackinaw City, MI 49701

Old Mackinac Point Light

Built: 1892
Style: Square Tower, Brick
Height: 49 feet (15m)

The Old Mackinac Point Light once guided sailors through the straits connecting Lake Michigan and Lake Huron on the Straits of Mackinac. It was originally erected as a fog signal station in 1890. However, after a series of foggy nights saw workers run the station for 327 hours straight and burning fifty-two cords of wood, government officials recognized the need for a bright beacon. Construction began and was finished in 1892.

This impressive site includes an original warehouse and the keepers quarters, with three rooms restored to reflect how lighthouse keepers lived in the early 1900s. Still on site are various original artifacts, including a Fresnel lens. The revolving lens produced a red flash of light every ten seconds and was connected by a clockwork mechanism that had to be wound up by hardworking keepers every three hours.

The Mackinac Island State Park Commission aided in efforts to restore the landmark so that it could be opened to the public in 1972. However, low attendance caused the site to shut its doors in 1990. But after a $2.2 million dollar fundraising effort, the lighthouse was reopened again in 1996. The site is nestled within Michilimackinac State Park, right on the shore of Lake Michigan.

LEFT & ABOVE: The Keeper's Quarters have been restored to its 1910 appearance. There is also a gallery exhibit on the history of the lighthouse which includes displays and artifacts. A brand new exhibit devoted to optics and lenses and fog signals is also situated here.

Point Betsie Light

Built: 1858
Style: Tower, Brick
Height: 36 feet (11m)

Point Betsie is the oldest standing structure in Benzie County. The name derives from a combination of Native American and French words. The lighthouse is a recognizable entrance point to the southern end of the Manitou Passage and was a key point for ships entering this area. It is still used as a navigational aid today.

Construction began in 1854 and continued over the next four years with a budget of only $5,000. Just months after the lighthouse was in full service, it was recognized that the sand around the lighthouse was causing the foundation to quickly erode. To better support the structure, a new foundation was laid in 1869. The site, after the lamp was affixed in 1875, was considered one of the earliest lifesaving stations in the area.

Attached to the tower is a two-story dwelling. This open-to-the-public landmark is one of the last lights on the Great Lakes that used a keeper. in 1996, the rotating lens mechanisms that operated the original Fresnel lens finally gave way. The light was removed and put on display. The current light on the tower is still used today for navigational purposes. It became automated in 1983 by the US Coast Guard.

HOW TO GET THERE

There is an admission fee to tour the lighthouse, which is open for tours from Memorial Day to Columbus Day. Take M-72W to Empire for about 22 miles. Take a left at M-22S. Follow M-22S to Point Betsie Road for about 17 miles. Turn right onto Point Betsie Road. The lighthouse is on your right.

Address
3701 Point Betsie Rd.
Frankfort, MI 49635

LEFT & ABOVE: Point Betsie is one of the finest and most photographed of all the historical lighthouses in the Great Lakes region.

HOW TO GET THERE

Tours are not available, but the lighthouse can be viewed from Point Beach State Park where a walking trail takes you fairly close to the structure. From WI-42, turn right on 22nd Street and then a slight left onto County Highway-O/Sandy Bay Road. Continue to follow County Highway-O until you see the beach and the lighthouse.

Address
Point Beach State Park
9400 County Rd. O
Two Rivers, WI 54241

Rawley Point Light

Built: 1894
Style: Skeletal Iron
Range: 19 miles (31km)
Height: 111 feet (34m)

Records show that twenty-six ships were destroyed on the rocks at Rawley Point before a lighthouse tower was constructed. The worst shipwreck claimed the lives of 36 sailors and passengers. To avoid future tragedies, a tower of brick was built on the site in 1853. But after an exhibit at the World's Fair in Chicago some years later, this tall, sprawling tower was relocated to the site in 1894, where it still stands today as the second tallest lighthouse in Wisconsin.

Originally called the Twin River Point lighthouse in its early days, this metal, sturdy tower suffers with little effort the whipping winds that gust across the coasts of Lake Michigan. A Fresnel lens was placed in the skeletal structure in 1920, making the tower electric. That lens would guide ships until 1952 when damaged prisms called for the removal of the antiquated light. Today a modern light functions within the metal tower, flashing its white light toward the water every fifteen seconds. The light is considered one of the brightest on the Great Lakes and is visible up to 19 miles. It still operates today from sunrise to sunset.

LEFT & RIGHT: The Rawley Point Light is a US Coast Guard residence within a state park. Views of the light can be obtained from the surrounding beach area, but the house and grounds are not open to the public.

St. Joseph North Pier Lights

Inner Light
Built: 1907
Style: Square, Steel
Height: 57 feet (17.37m)

Outer Light
Built: 1907
Style: Conical Tower, Cast Iron
Height: 35 feet (10.66m)

The Saint Joseph North Pier Lights are two separate towers with their own distinct beacons. They stand several hundred feet apart but are connected by a sturdy, well-lit catwalk. The towers function together as "range lights." This is done purposefully so that ship navigators can keep them lined up with one behind the other in order to reach the harbor safely. The outer lighthouse is topped with a 10-sided lantern room.

The first lighthouse at the mouth of the St. Joseph River was built on a bluff in 1832 and again in 1859. It was a conical, rubblestone tower with a soapstone deck and octagonal lantern room. 1859 is also when the second tower was constructed. Both were rebuilt in 1907 to what they are now. Records show that lighthouse keeper Daniel R. Platt was the longest serving keeper at St. Joseph. He began in 1883, wrapping up his tenure in 1919. Platt held his post longer than most lighthouse keepers of his time.

Throughout the years, many efforts were put forth to save the original lighthouse and keeper's house on the bluff, but those efforts failed and the structures were destroyed. Things shifted, however, in 2014 after a committee was formed and raised $2 million dollars in private funds to save and preserve the two lighthouses. Preservation and restoration efforts continue today.

HOW TO GET THERE

These lighthouses are not open to the public but are accessible via the beach on the north side of the river. To get to the beach, take MI-63 and veer onto the Whitwan Drive ramp. Turn left on Whitwan, and then right on Upton Drive. From here, take a sharp left turn on Marina Drive. See Ridgeway Street on your left.

Address
Tiscornia Beach
80 Ridgeway St.
St. Joseph, MI 49085

RIGHT: The St. Joseph Pier Lights present such a pretty picture that they are often used as subjects by artists and photographers, and have even been featured on postage stamps. Their more serious purpose, however, is to guide vessels safely into the harbor.

HOW TO GET THERE

The tower is open to the public from Memorial Day to Labor Day. It is located five miles north of Harrisville on Lake Huron. Take US-23 north from Harrisville. Turn right onto Point Road. See the parking lot for the lighthouse less than a half mile down the road.

Address
6071 Point Rd.
Harrisville, MI 48740

Sturgeon Point Light

Built: 1869
Style: Conical, Brick
Height: 72 feet (22m)

In 1857 a lighthouse on Tawas point wasn't strong enough to light the fifty-five-mile gap between it and a second light on nearby Thunder Bay Island. To illuminate the gap, the Lighthouse Board proposed a tower be erected at the midpoint. And so in 1869, this massive brick tower was built in an effort to save many lives from a once unseen nearby jagged reef.

Eighty-five steps take visitors to the top where they can get a bird's eye view of the western shore of Lake Huron. The tower originally housed a Fresnel lens that was shipped from the lighthouse in Oswego, New York. The attached keepers' house is also made of brick.

In 1913 the US Coast Guard retired the last lighthouse keeper that would man the mighty tower. For a short while, the captain of the nearby lifesaving station lived there with his family. After they moved on, the site remained vacant, save a few vandals that found their way onto the property. In 1982, the Alcona Historical Society assumed the responsibility of the site with the intention to refurbish it and bring it back to its original state. Dozens of volunteers and historical workers labored diligently over a three year period to restore the keeper's house and lighthouse, painting both structures their original colors of white and red.

LEFT: Sturgeon Point's powerful beacon still warns shipping of the presence of dangerous shoals, but now the residence houses a museum.

Tawas Point Light

Built: 1876
Style: Conical, Brick
Height: 67 feet (17.37m)

Like the Sturgeon Point Light, this particular light was very much needed, especially after Saginaw Bay on Lake Huron saw extensive growth with commercial ships in the mid-1800s. To mark the entrance of the bay, lighthouse officials placed a light on the south side in 1848. Another was placed on the north side in 1853. This north side light was the original Tawas Point light and served its purpose until officials appropriated funds to build a new one in 1876. As with most lighthouses in the area, it was topped with a Fresnel lens.

The first lighthouse keeper to man the tower was Sherman Wheeler. He made $350 a year and lived in a nearby a five-room keepers' house with an attached kitchen. After the house and tower fell into disrepair, funds were approved for a new one. In 1876, the current standing structure was built.

The light, originally known as Ottawa Point, functioned for years and saw many different transformations. Over the years sand caused erosion, which required many updates. Because the tower was so far inland, it was said that the light atop the tower was too dim, and was responsible for shipwrecks that could have otherwise been avoided. After the schooner Dolphin was destroyed, Congress approved funding for a new lighthouse. This is the lighthouse that stands today.

BELOW: Originally known as Ottawa Point, the lighthouse's name was officially changed to Tawas Point in 1902.

HOW TO GET THERE

Tours of the Tawas Point Lighthouse are available May through September. The lighthouse is located southeast of East Tawas in Tawas Point State Park, just off US-23. Turn right onto Tawas Beach Road. Continue to the parking area and follow the walking path toward the lighthouse.

Address
686 Tawas Beach Rd.
East Tawas, MI 48730

LIGHTHOUSES OF THE NORTHEAST

The waters on the East Coast of North America were once a superhighway for ships and vessels carrying much-needed goods and commodities. Here, strong currents lapped at the coastline, making the sea lanes high risk. As a result, many a wreck can be found below the waters here. But many, many more were guided safely, thanks to the lighthouses of the northeast.

ANNISQUAM HARBOR LIGHT

Built: 1897
Style: Cylindrical, Brick
Range: 14 miles (26km)
Height: 41 feet (12.5m)

This lighthouse is legendary in New England for various reasons. Not only has it served maritime sailors over the years, but it was also the backdrop for the 2008 film *The Women,* starring Meg Ryan and Annette Bening. In the late 1950s, the lighthouse and its keeper were featured in an insurance advertisement in *Time Magazine*. However, all fame aside, this landmark holds a part of history that goes deeper than films and magazines.

The 1801 tower and station that mark this site was known originally known as Wigwam Point. The first tower constructed was 32-feet tall, and it was erected to illuminate Squam Bar. Built with a two-room dwelling near the tower, the site was manned by a Gloucester native by the name of James Day. His annual salary to keep the stationary light working was a meager $200 a year.

In 1897, the wooden tower was replaced with its current cylinder tower. The light was electrified in 1974, relieving the last lightkeeper at Annisquam Harbor. Eventually, the Coast Guard deactivated the iconic fog horn, but area fisherman and townsfolk wouldn't have it. A petition was circulated to have the horn turned back on. In the end, it was reinstated but relocated at a nearby police station.

HOW TO GET THERE

The lighthouse is not open to the public but can be viewed from Wingaersheek Beach. To get to the beach, take Route 128 north to Exit 13. Turn left off the ramp onto Concord Street. Continue until you see a traffic island with a Wingaersheek Beach sign. Turn right onto Atlantic Street and follow to the end.

Address
Wingaersheek Beach
Atlantic St.
Gloucester, MA 01930

RIGHT: Owned by the US Coast Guard, Annisquam Harbor Light Station is still an active aid to navigation. In 2000, a major restoration of the tower was conducted by the Coast Guard.

BASS HARBOR HEAD LIGHT

Built: 1858
Style: Cylindrical, Brick
Range: 13 miles (24km)
Height: 32 feet (9.75m)

BELOW LEFT & BELOW: The highly photogenic Bass Harbor Head Light, perched on its colored rocks, is one of a cluster of historic lighthouses located in the vicinity of Mount Desert and Acadia National Park.

The Bass Harbor Head lighthouse sits atop a rocky ledge on Mount Desert Island in its original form, still guiding ships into Blue Hill Bay and Bass Harbor today. This island is the largest off the coast of Maine, covering 108 square miles. The light flashes every four seconds, sending red illumination over the rocks and waters below.

HOW TO GET THERE

The lighthouse is closed to the public but can be viewed from Arcadia National Park. Head south on Highway 3 toward Acadia National Park. It will turn into Highway 198. Turn left on Highway 102 and continue onto Highway 102A. Continue straight on Lighthouse Road.

Address
Arcadia National Park
39 Lighthouse Rd.
Tremont, ME 04634

Originally, there was no easy access to the tower from the water. A boat landing and boathouse were added in 1894, so that mariners could come ashore and supplies could be transported with greater ease up the rocks to the keeper's house.

The house itself was constructed with a covered walkway to help protect the keeper and his family during harsh storms. The original dwelling was two stories with five rooms. An outhouse was also built on site. Drinking water for the family was collected by catching rainwater from the roof and stored in an 1,800 gallon tub.

A Fresnel lens was installed in the tower in 1902 but was replaced in 1974 to make way for an electric light. The lighthouse and foghorn are still active under the watch of the US Coast Guard today.

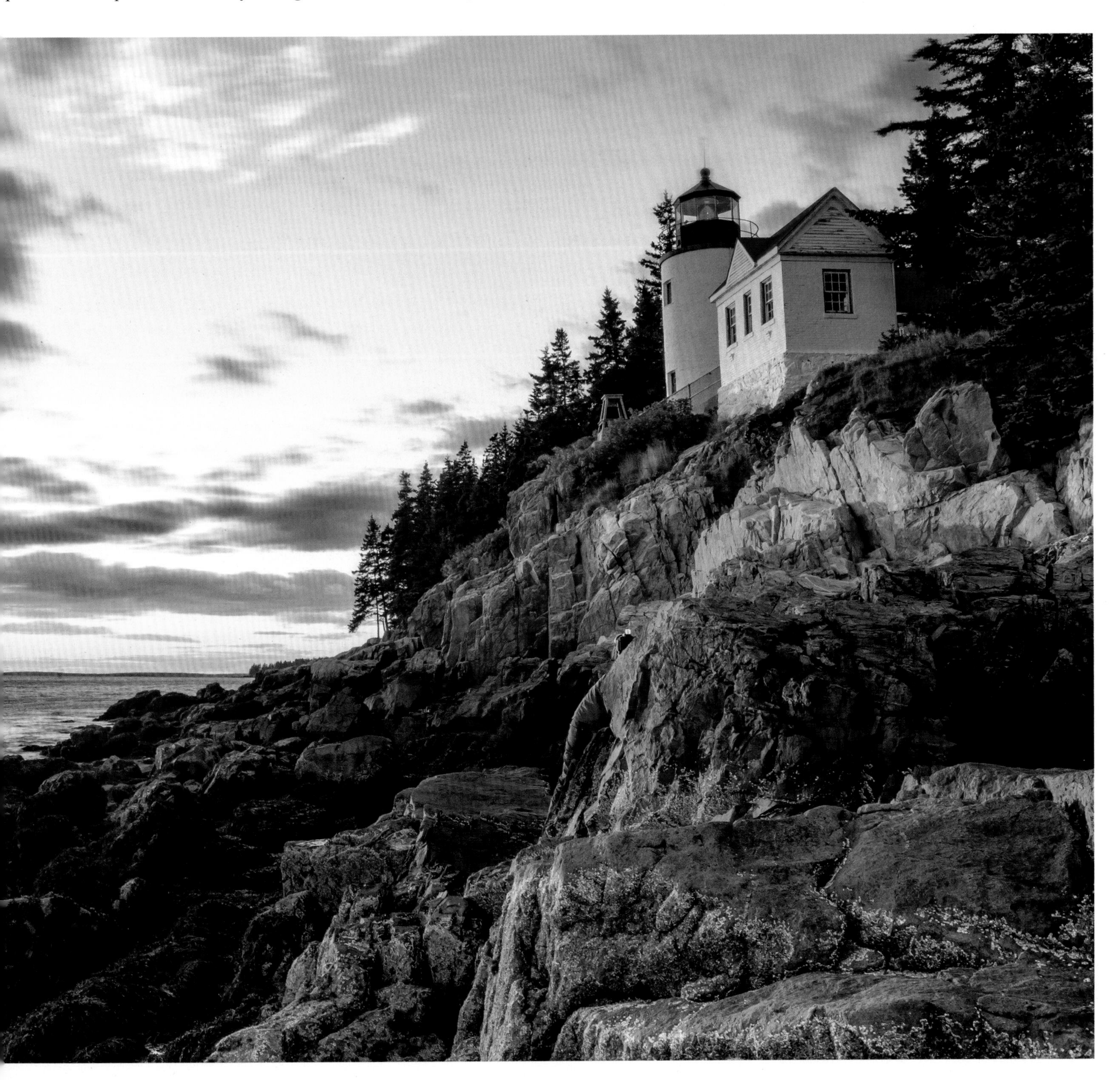

BRANT POINT LIGHT

Style: Salt Shaker Style
Range: 10 miles (19km)
Height: 26 feet (7.92m)

Considered America's second oldest light station, this legendary light was built after sea captains proposed it be constructed during a town hall meeting in January 1746. The proposal was approved and the light erected at the entrance of Nantucket Harbor three months later. However, it was shipping taxes that paid for the lighthouse, which didn't make the wanting sea captains very happy.

This lighthouse, along with at least half a dozen others that were rebuilt in the same location, met their demise by fire or damaging wind and water. The first fire was in 1758. The tower was rebuilt fairly quickly but was met with tragedy again when it was knocked over by gale force winds in 1774. A new light was erected, but fire claimed it in 1783. It was replaced with a wooden lantern that emitted poor light. Townsfolk and mariners dubbed it the "bug light," it was so dim. But it didn't last long. Fire struck again in 1786. Once again, the light was replaced. This one only lasted two years because, in 1788, a fierce storm took it down.

A few more towers would be constructed before the current tower was built to outlast all others. The light was automated in 1965. The original Fresnel lens, installed in 1856, can be viewed at the Nantucket Life Saving Museum. Restorations in 2000 brought the lighthouse to its current state.

HOW TO GET THERE

The lighthouse is closed to the public but can be viewed from the north side of Nantucket Island. To get there, start at the Steamboat Wharf and head up Broad Street. Turn right onto South Beach Street and then right onto Easton Street. At the end of the street, park in the lot at Hulbert Avenue.

Address
2 Easton St.
Nantucket, MA 02554

RIGHT: Brant Point Light is located on Nantucket Island. It was first built in 1746. Since then, it has had many reincarnations, the present lighthouse dating from 1901. It was automated in 1965 and is still in operation. It was added to the National Register of Historic Places in October 1987.

CAPE NEDDICK LIGHT

Built: 1879
Style: Cylindrical, Cast Iron
Range: 13 miles (24km)
Height: 41 feet (12.5m)

Marking the entrance of the York River, this lighthouse, also affectionately called "The Nubble," has some interesting bits of history. Built on a small, rocky island, it earned its nickname from local fisherman. And while the name was endearing to locals, the pay that lighthouse keepers received was not.

Long before lighthouses were historic landmarks to be toured, it was learned that some lighthouse keepers were making money "on the side" to supplement their meager incomes. At Cape Neddick, lighthouse keeper William Brooks gave tours of the grounds during the day for 10 cents per person. His wife gave tours of the house for a nickel. Upon discovery by the government, they were promptly fired.

This lighthouse has seen outer space, too. When the Voyager spacecraft launched in 1977, a picture of Maine's Cape Neddick was on board. It was included as a prominent landmark to help life in other galaxies identify Earth.

The light on the tower was automated in 1987. Today, it attracts visitors year round. One of the biggest draws to the lighthouse is the annual Lighting of the Nubble when the Town of York dress the buildings with Christmas lights in November. While the lighthouse itself is not accessible to the public, the entire site is a popular backdrop for weddings.

BELOW & RIGHT: The Cape Neddick Light stands on a craggy outcrop, known as the Nubble, situated just off the cape. It was completed in 1879 and remains in excellent condition. Over Christmas the light is lit up.

HOW TO GET THERE

From the east in York, take Route 1A (also Long Beach Avenue) to Nubble Road. Head down the road for about a mile until you reach Sohier Park. You'll see the lighthouse at this point. There is free parking at the end of the road.

Address
Sohier Park
Sohier Park Rd.
York, ME 03909

CHATHAM LIGHT

Built: 1808
Style: Cylindrical, Brick
Height: 43 feet (13.1m)

President Thomas Jefferson appointed the first keeper of this lard-burning lighthouse to guide ships on Cape Cod. When President Zachary Taylor was in office, he promised the position to a patronage appointee. At the time, the tower was kept by the widow of lighthouse keeper Simeon Nickerson. Thanks to public outcry, the appointment was dismissed and the widow, Angeline, was able to keep the job and provide for her children. She remained at her post for the next ten years.

The Chatham light was of seven "twin" lights in North America. Originally a twin light on the north Atlantic coast, it was erected in 1808 to distinguish it from nearby Highland Light, which was erected two years earlier. So that the lighthouses could be distinguished from one another, Chatham was equipped with two towers with white lights. The towers stood 70 feet apart from one another. The keeper's nearby house was tiny, with only one bedroom. Rebuilt once in 1841 and again in 1977, Chatham was separated from Highland in 1923. The light is still active today under the watchful eye of the US Coast Guard.

"Darkness reigns at the foot of the lighthouse."

Japanese Proverb

RIGHT: The waters surrounding Cape Cod have a plethora of warning beacons–so many in fact that, in the early 19th century, mariners had difficulty identifying them. In 1808, officials conceived the idea of marking the channel leading to Chatham harbor with a double light. Today, the Chatham beacon is now illuminated through a modern optic.

HOW TO GET THERE

The lighthouse is closed to the public, save the occasional summer tour. From Route 6, take Exit 11 toward Chatham on Route 137 and head south. Turn left onto Old Queen Anne Road. After 1 mile, turn right again to stay on Old Queen Anne Road. From there, make a left onto Main Street. Next, make a right onto School Street, then a quick left onto Water Street. Make one more right onto Silver Leaf Avenue.

Address
Chatham Lighthouse Beach
37 Main St.
Chatham, MA 02633

EAST POINT LIGHT

Built: 1867
Style: Cape-Cod Home, Octagonal Tower
Height: 65 feet (19.81m)

East Point Light has played an important part in the maritime history in the Maurice River area of Cumberland County, New Jersey. Originally known as the Maurice River Light, it was erected in 1849 by the United States Lighthouse Establishment, the present name having been initiated in 1913. Throughout the years, its guiding light has shown fishermen, oystermen, and recreational boaters the way into the mouth of the Maurice River and, during daylight hours, has been used as a landmark by hunters, trappers, and surveyors.

Although numerous lighthouses once stood along the edge of the Delaware Bay, East Point is the last one remaining on the Jersey side. In fact, it is the second oldest lighthouse standing in New Jersey (only the Sandy Hook Lighthouse of 1764 is older).

The US Coast Guard operated the East Point Light from 1939 until 1941 when the light was extinguished due to the beginning of the World War II. In 1956 the property was deeded to the New Jersey Division of Fish, Game, and Wildlife. Over the years the vacant structure suffered greatly from vandalism and weather, but in early 1971 a group of concerned local citizens formed the Maurice River Historical Society, with the goal of saving the historic building from destruction. In July of that year, an incident occurred which nearly doomed the lighthouse; a trespasser in the building caused a fire which destroyed the roof and the lantern room.

In the mid 1970s, funded only by local fundraising and donations, determined members of the Maurice River Historical Society succeeded in rebuilding the roof and lantern room. Then, on July 2, 1980, at public request, the US Coast Guard reinstalled a beacon in the structure and put the East Point Light back on its list of active navigational aids.

BELOW & OPPOSITE: The lantern room offers a panoramic view of the surrounding land and water, and it is a favorite subject of photographers and painters alike.

HOW TO GET THERE

Tours are available the first and third weekend of each month. There is an admittance fee. From the Garden State Parkway, take exit 13 to Avalon Blvd. Turn right onto Route 9 and then left onto Route 83. After four miles, Route 83 will merge with Route 47. Bear right onto Route 47. Travel about ten miles through Delmont. Turn left onto Glade Road. Glade Road eventually turns into East Point Road, which becomes Lighthouse Road.

Address
10 Lighthouse Rd.
Heislerville, NJ 08324

EDGARTOWN HARBOR LIGHT

Built: 1828
Style: Cast Iron
Height: 45 feet (13.71m)

The first lighthouse to grace the jagged rocks on Chappaquiddick Island was connected to the mainland by a wooden walkway. Built in 1830, the 1,500 walkway cost $2,500 to build. It was efficient and useful until fierce winds and damaging water brought it and the original tower down in a hurricane in 1938. Officials planned on replacing the tower with a steel skeleton tower, but financing the construction was an issue. Instead, a vacant lighthouse constructed in 1881 was dismantled and barged over from Crane's Island in Ipswich.

More wind and rain wore the structure down over time. But, as is the case with most of these iconic, slender castles, it was restored. Thanks to a $250,000 grant received by the Martha's Vineyard Historical Society, restoration began in 2007. Rusted bolts were replaced with new ones. The unsturdy ladder to the top was replaced with a spiral staircase. And new windows preserved the view from the top. The light in Martha's Vineyard is owned by the US Coast Guard and leased to the Martha's Vineyard Historical Society.

BELOW & OPPOSITE: Over the decades, sand has gradually filled in the area between the lighthouse and the mainland. Therefore, Edgartown Harbor Light is now located on the beach, and it continues to operate as an active aid to navigation.

HOW TO GET THERE

The lighthouse is open to the public on weekends May through September. For the tour, there is an admission fee. It is also available for group visits and private rentals. There is no parking available. It is recommended that visitors take The Vineyard Transit Authority (VTA) to Church Street in Edgartown, and then make the 10-minute walk to the lighthouse on North Water Street.

Address
121 North Water St.
Edgartown, MA 02539

FIRE ISLAND LIGHT

Built: 1858
Style: Cylindrical, Brick
Range: 24 miles (38.62km)
Height: 167 feet (50.9m)

Fire Island Light likely got its name for the fires that were built on the shores in the 19th century to help guide ships. Although, some historians believe it was dubbed this because pirates lit fires to lure unsuspecting ships to the island so they could pillage the cargo. One other theory is that the island got its name because of a large amount of poison ivy there.

ABOVE & RIGHT: The Fire Island Light originally stood only 200 yards from the western edge of the island, but miles of beach have been added to the island during the past century or more.

No matter the origin of its name, Fire Island is considered the most important lighthouse site for transatlantic steamers coming into the New York Harbor.

The original structure, built in 1826, stood only 74 feet tall. However, it wasn't tall enough to accommodate incoming ships. The Lighthouse

Board recognized this and so ordered a taller tower be constructed. The stone from the original tower was used to build the terrace of the present tower, yet it took another 80,000 bricks to complete it. Visitors take 192 steps to the top, stopping every twenty-six to peek through a window at the land and waters below.

The beacon was lit until 1974, when it was shut off for the last time. For years, the tower fell into disrepair until the Fire Island Preservation Society formed in 1982 to bring it back to life. By 1986, the lighthouse was back in service.

HOW TO GET THERE

The lighthouse is open to the public at various times throughout the year. There is an admission fee. It is also available for weddings and other events. To get there, take Southern Parkway to exit 40 south. Turn onto Sunrise Highway and take exit 41S. This is the Robert Moses Causeway. The lighthouse is east of Robert Moses State Park off the causeway. You can park in field #5.

Address
4640 Captree Island
Captree Island, NY 11702

HENDRICKS HEAD LIGHT

Built: 1875
Style: Federal Style, Brick
Height: 40 feet (12.19m)

The original lighthouse on Southport Island near Boothbay Harbor in Maine was built in 1829 to assist in guiding vessels up Sheepscot River. It was the first whale oil-fired light to be used in the area. By 1875 the lighthouse was, per to the Lighthouse Board, in "an advanced state of dilapidation." It was torn down and a new lighthouse and detached keeper's house was constructed that same year.

Every lighthouse has a rich history and many remarkable stories to go with it. For Hendricks Head in Boothbay Harbor, the story of a child washed ashore is one that is truly remarkable. During a fierce snowstorm in the 1860s it is said that the keeper pulled an ice-covered mattress from the waters. He was stunned to find a crying baby clinging to life inside. Attached to the baby was a note from the captain of a nearby sinking schooner. To try and spare the baby, the captain released the child to the waters. The keeper acted fast to save the child, and he and his wife raised the tiny baby as their own.

Today the lighthouse is privately owned by Ben and Luanne Russell of Alabama. It underwent a complete renovation by the couple in 1993 to near-perfect condition.

HOW TO GET THERE

The lighthouse is privately owned but can be seen from the beach in West Southport. From US Highway 1, cross the bridge at Wiscasset and take Route 27 through Boothbay Harbor to Southport Island. Turn right on Lakeside Drive. Turn right at the grocery store onto Beech Road. Go about three miles until you see the lighthouse.

Address
Lighthouse Lane
Southport, ME 04576

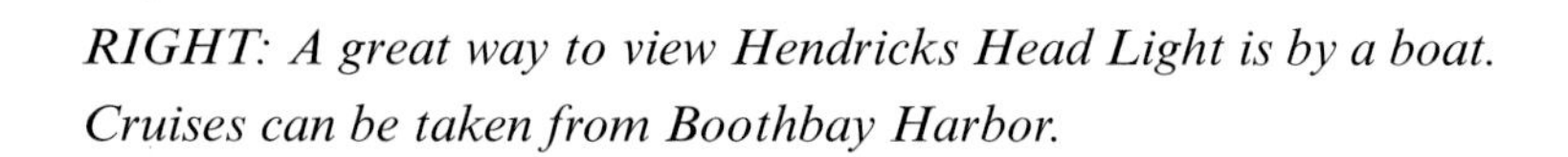

RIGHT: A great way to view Hendricks Head Light is by a boat. Cruises can be taken from Boothbay Harbor.

HYANNIS HARBOR LIGHT

Built: 1849
Style: Colonial
Height: 19 feet (5.8m)

Tucked away on a side street, the Hyannis Harbor Light, also known as the South Hyannis Light, goes unnoticed by most of the tourists who come to the area to take a ferry to Nantucket or Martha's Vineyard, or to catch a glimpse of the Kennedy farmily's Hyannisport compound. The privately owned lighthouse and keeper's house has been altered so much through the decades that only an informed visitor would recognize what was once an important light station.

The original lighthouse was a mere shack, with a lamp and reflector borrowed from Point Gammon. Given that this was a busy harbor in the 19th century, the government decided to establish a lighthouse, this being a small, white tower at the harbor entrance in 1849. A keeper's house was constructed in 1850, and a Fresnel lens installed in 1856.

In 1885 a range light was added on the nearby Old Colony Railroad Wharf, this being a simple lamp hoisted to the top of a 20-ft (6-m) wooden tower. The new range light and the lighthouse would be lined up by mariners as a guide to Hyannis Harbor. Railroad cars would often be left in a position that blocked the range light, and keeper John Peak would have to remonstrate with railroad personnel until they move the cars. The tower was rebuilt in 1886 due to the fact that the range light often extinguished itself during storms. An oil house was added in 1889.

The lantern room was removed and the lighthouse was decommissioned in 1929. It was sold to private individuals, who build an enlarged lantern room atop the tower for use as a sitting room.

HOW TO GET THERE

The lighthouse is private property and is not visible from the street (do not trespass). The best viewing location is from a small park on Ocean Avenue just to the west of the lighthouse. From the intersection of Highways 132 and 28 north of Hyannis, turn south on Hyannis-Barnstable Road. In Hyannis, continue south on Ocean Street to Gosnold Street. Turn right on Gosnold Street and drive to Harbor Road. Turn left on Harbor Road, where the lighthouse will be on your right near the end of the road.

Address
Harbor Rd.
Hyannis, MA 02601

RIGHT: The original the bird-cage style lantern was removed in 1863 and replaced with the larger cast-iron lantern seen today.

MARSHALL POINT LIGHT

Built: 1857
Style: Colonial Revival, Brick & Granite
Height: 31 feet (9.44m)

Just about every lighthouse has a predecessor that no longer exists in any form. For the Marshall Point Light, its predecessor was erected in 1832, constructed to mark the entrance of Port Clyde. But poor construction gave it short life, and in 1857 a new tower was built with brick and granite. The keeper's house, however, was not, and succumbed to a lightning storm in 1895 that destroyed most of it. Repairs were made to make it liveable while a new dwelling was constructed next to it.

Marshall Point was a breakthrough station in that it was one of the first to be connected to a weather station by phone. This allowed keepers

ABOVE & RIGHT: Marshall Point Light offers a safe haven to mariners entering the tiny fishing village of Port Clyde.

to display storm warning flags on a nearby mast. A more relevant fact, the tower can be seen in the beloved film, *Forrest Gump* as he runs cross-country in one of the most iconic sequences in the film. Today, the site is fully restored with the lighthouse, a connected walkway, and a two-story keeper's dwelling.

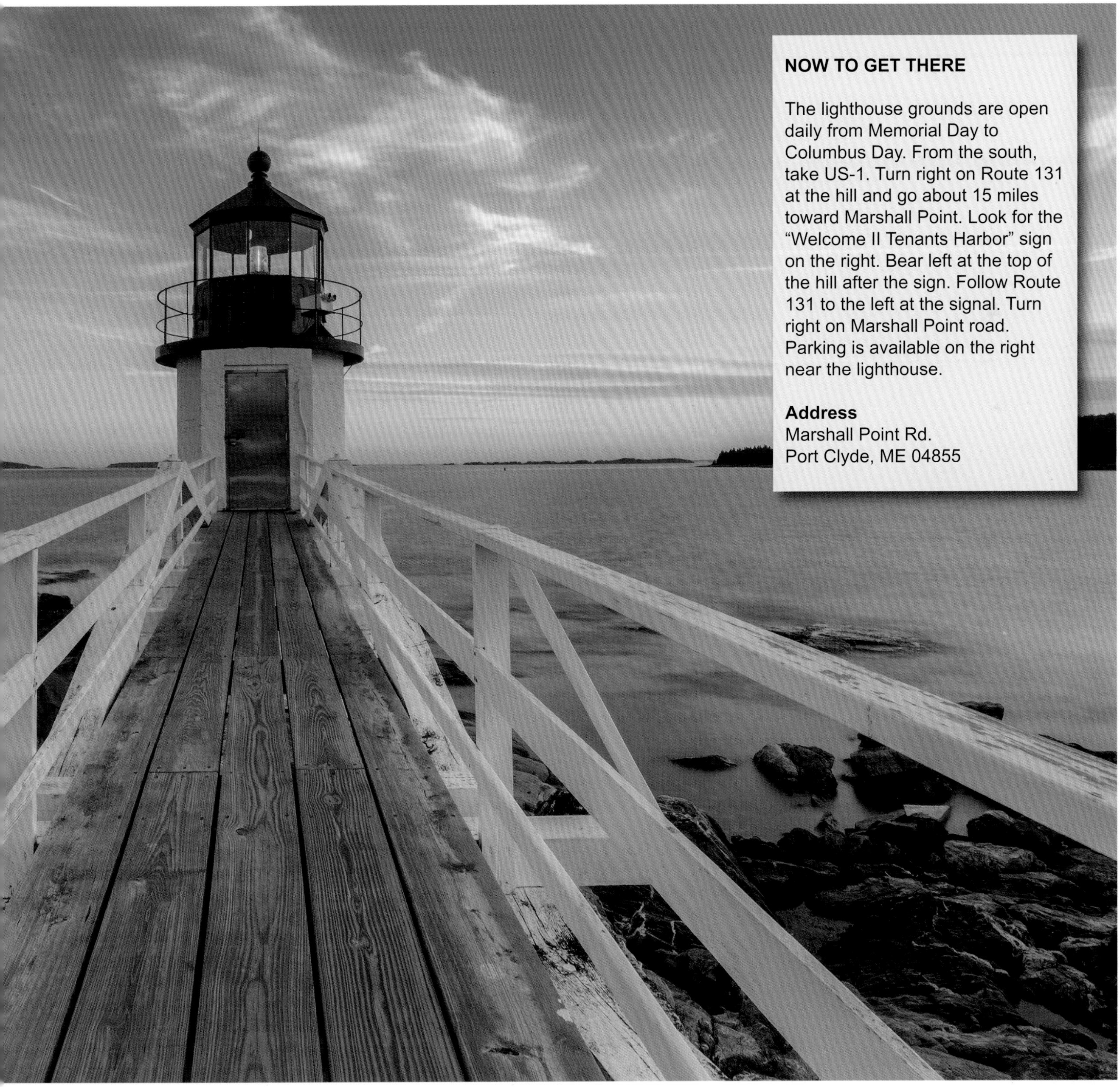

NOW TO GET THERE

The lighthouse grounds are open daily from Memorial Day to Columbus Day. From the south, take US-1. Turn right on Route 131 at the hill and go about 15 miles toward Marshall Point. Look for the "Welcome II Tenants Harbor" sign on the right. Bear left at the top of the hill after the sign. Follow Route 131 to the left at the signal. Turn right on Marshall Point road. Parking is available on the right near the lighthouse.

Address
Marshall Point Rd.
Port Clyde, ME 04855

MONTAUK POINT LIGHT

Built: 1796
Style: Octagonal, Sandstone
Range: 18 miles (29km)
Height: 111 feet (33.83m)

The first lights to burn at Montauk Point were fires created by the Indians to call their chiefs and other warriors to council. In these early days, the point was referred to as Turtle Hill because settlers thought the point was shaped like a turtle's shell. The US government recognized the usefulness of lighting the point and decided it should be illuminated with an actual lighthouse for navigational purposes. Therefore, in 1796, Montauk Point Light was erected. The tower, along with a two-story keeper's dwelling, is the original structure that was built over 200 years ago.

This legendary lighthouse is the oldest in New York State. Enduring fierce Atlantic storms, this iconic light was a welcome sight for immigrants headed for New York. For decades, the lamps on the tower burned whale oil. Later, it was switched to lard and then kerosene. The light was automated in 1987. It became a museum for curious visitors that same year.

BELOW & RIGHT: The Montauk Point Light is located in Montauk Point State Park. The lighthouse was the first to be built within the state of New York.

HOW TO GET THERE

The lighthouse is open to the public with an admission fee. To get there, head east on I-495 to County Road 111 at exit 70. Then, head south on Route 27 (Sunrise Highway) toward Montauk State Park. Parking is available at the state park.

Address
2000 Montauk Hwy.
Montauk, NY 11954

NANTUCKET LIGHT (Great Point Light)

Built: 1784
Style: Conical, Stone
Height: 70 feet (21.33m)

Established in 1784, the Great Point Light of Nantucket (also known as the Nantucket Lighthouse) was once central to one of the busiest navigational areas on the East Coast, thanks to a thriving whaling industry. To help ships navigate the waterways, Captain Paul Pinkham, one of the light's first keepers, created the first accurate map of New England's coast in 1790. This made it clear that Great Point was a crucial gateway and needed to be understood better in order to avoid shipwrecks and the like. Despite the captain's best efforts and the efforts of the Lighthouse Board, one keeper noted in a journal that between the years of 1863 and 1890, forty-three shipwrecks were recorded. The primary cause of the shipwrecks was that Great Point was so often mistaken for the Cross Rip and Handkerchief Shoal Lightships nearby.

The light itself sits stoically at the tip of a sand strip some seven miles long, overlooking the gap between Nantucket and Monomoy Islands. Fire was not a friend to the island in the early days. In 1812, the keeper's house caught fire. And then, after years of steadfastness, the wooden tower was destroyed by a suspicious fire in 1818. It was rebuilt with stone the same year.

Still not done with danger, the lighthouse was toppled over by a hurricane in 1984. Discussion to replace it with a relocated fiberglass tower were nixed by Massachusetts Senator Edward M. Kennedy, who secured federal monies to rebuild the light. The new tower was finished and dedicated in 1986.

HOW TO GET THERE

The lighthouse is not typically open to the public, but tours can be organized by contacting the Coskata-Coatue Wildlife Refuge. Some visitors have taken a Jeep to reach the remote location. To get to the refuge from the Nantucket town rotary, take Polpis Road east for about six miles and then turn left onto Wauwinet Road. Continue to the gatehouse. There is no parking area.

Address
Coskata-Coatue Wildlife Refuge
107 Wauwinet Rd.
Nantucket, MA 02554

RIGHT: Nantucket Light is situated on a thin spit of beach where the currents of the Atlantic Ocean and Nantucket Sound meet.

NAUSET BEACH LIGHT

Built: 1838
Style: Cylindrical, Cast Iron
Height: 49 feet (14.93m)

This particular beacon and tower has seen many transformations over the years, thanks to shifting shorelines and poorly constructed lighthouses. The original site was built with three lights in three adjacent towers to differentiate from the twin lights at Chatham and Cape Cod, Truro. The towers stood only 15 feet tall and were referred to by sailors as the "Three Sisters." Because they were too close to the beach, the trio of towers suffered erosion and eventually toppled to the sand in 1892.

They were rebuilt as wooden towers and moved further inland. But they still proved inefficient. Two decades later, two of the towers were removed. The third remaining tower stayed, but was again moved away from the shore to avoid further erosion. When this tower began to fall into disrepair, officials decided to dismantle it and relocate one of the former Chatham lights to the site.

The Coast Guard decommissioned the light in 1993, but the public wanted to see it preserved. The issue was that the coast had eroded even more, leaving the lighthouse dangerously close to the edge of the cliff. But in 1996 it was moved across the road to where it sits now, well preserved as a historic landmark in Cape Cod.

RIGHT & INSET: The lighthouse pictured here began life in 1881 as one of Chatham's twin lights. In 1923, this, Chatham's north tower, was moved to Nauset Beach, where it replaced Nauset's original Three Sisters lights, built by Winslow Lewis in 1838.

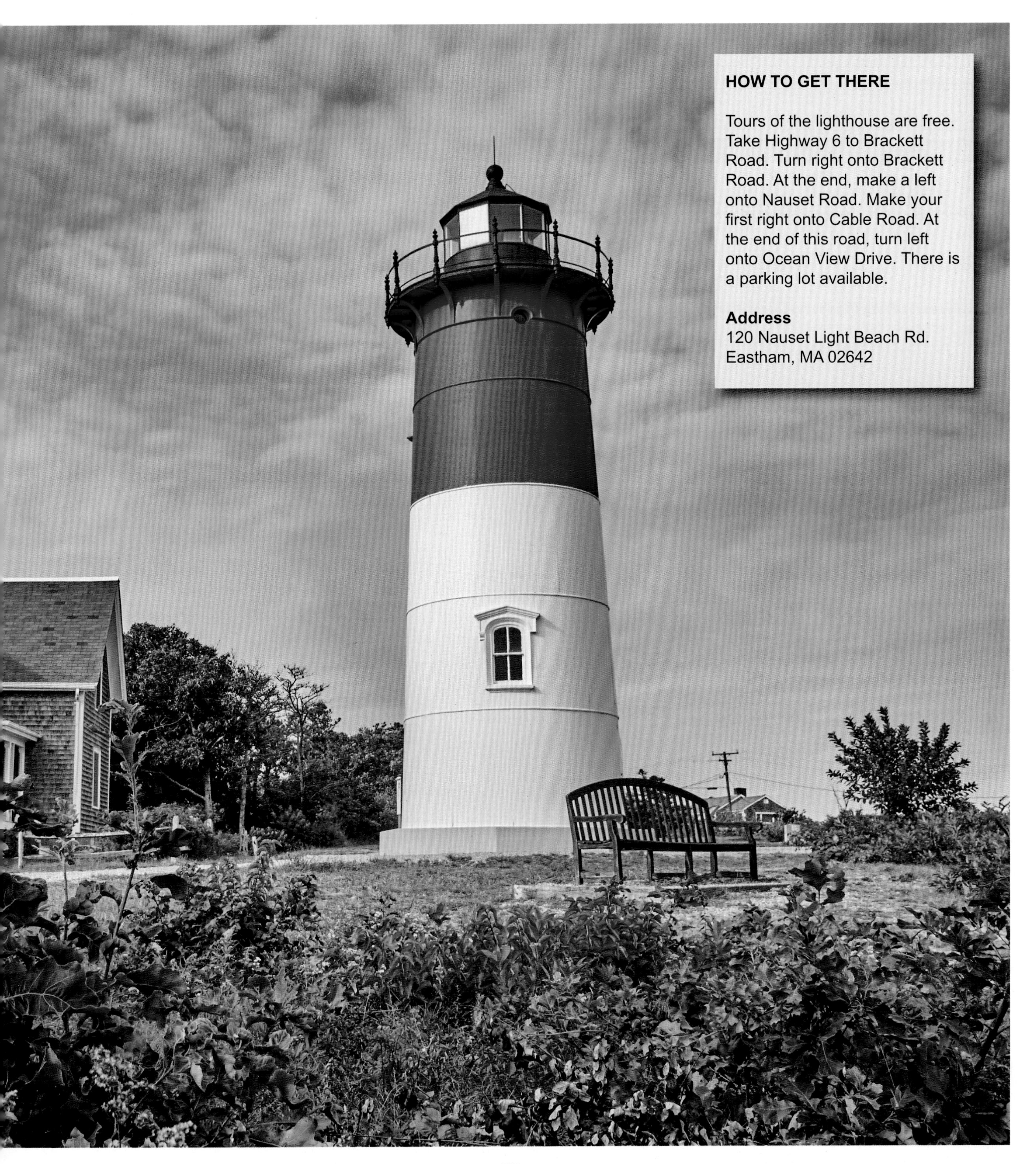

HOW TO GET THERE

Tours of the lighthouse are free. Take Highway 6 to Brackett Road. Turn right onto Brackett Road. At the end, make a left onto Nauset Road. Make your first right onto Cable Road. At the end of this road, turn left onto Ocean View Drive. There is a parking lot available.

Address
120 Nauset Light Beach Rd.
Eastham, MA 02642

NOBSKA POINT LIGHT

Built: 1828
Style: Cast Iron, Brick Lining
Height: 40 feet (12.19m)

Nobska Point Light was known as the Nobsque Point Light when it was originally built in 1828. It was a wooden structure with keeper's quarters. In 1841 the popular Fresnel lens was installed. According to then lightkeeper Peter Dagget, the oil lamps burned close to 340 gallons of oil a year, all of which had to be laboriously carried up the stairs daily.

BELOW LEFT & BELOW: The Nobska (Nobsque) Light is located at the southwestern tip of Cape Cod, between Buzzard's Bay and Vineyard Sound. The original structure was a design common at the time, being a lantern room installed on the roof of a residence, but it was too heavy and caused the light's roof to leak. The present Nobska Light dates from 1876 and is made of steel. It still has a Fresnel lens, which beams a white light. The light was automated in 1985.

HOW TO GET THERE

The lighthouse is not open to the public at this time, but can be viewed from the beach, southeast of Woods Hole Village in the town of Falmouth, Cape Cod. From Boston, take Route 93 south to Route 3 south. Go over the Sagamore Bridge to Route 6 west. From there, follow signs from the Bourne Bridge.

Address
233 Nobska Rd.
Woods Hole, MA 02543

In 1876 the failing tower was replaced by the current tower. As far as lighthouse keepers go, records show that the Nobska Point Light was operated by the US Lighthouse Service from 1828 until 1939. But service of keepers didn't end there. Joseph Hindley was the last to man the tower, retiring from his post in 1972.

The light is still active today, maintained by the US Coast Guard. It flashes every six seconds with two fog signal blasts every 30 seconds. Up until 2013, the dwelling was home to a US Coast Guard officer. Restoration on the lighthouse continues under the watchful eye of a non-profit organization called Friends of Nobska Light. Upgrades began in 2017 and are ongoing. Completion of the tower and museum are slated for 2020.

PEMAQUID POINT LIGHT

Built: 1835
Style: Cylindrical, Stone
Height: 38 feet (11.58m)

Originally commissioned in 1827 by John Quincy Adams, the Pemaquid Point Light sits on a stretch of striated rock that was a danger to ships passing through the thick fog at Muscongus Bay in Maine. Shipwrecks here weren't uncommon. To avoid them further, the light was constructed. It was rebuilt in 1857 and equipped with a Fresnel lens. Sometime in 1897, an engine house was erected to run a new fog bell. It

HOW TO GET THERE

Located at the entrance to Muscongus Bay and Johns Bay, the lighthouse is open to the public for a small admission fee. Cruises nearby can also take visitors past the lighthouse. From US Highway 1 at Damariscotta, take Route 130 for about 16 miles to the lighthouse.

Address
3115 Bristol Rd.
Bristol, ME 04558

was steam powered and installed to replace the original bell that keeper's rung by hand.

Even with lights and fog horns, dangers on the sea are inevitable. In 1927 at Pemaquid Point, the lighthouse keeper was forced to head into the choppy waters to rescue a teenage boy who washed up on shore. The 68-year-old keeper couldn't revive him, but was able to save his aunt and

uncle still in the waters. This heroic act wouldn't be the last. After the keeper retired his post, the station's next and final keeper, Leroy S. Elwell, saved three people from a boat that capsized during poor weather.

Pemaquid Point is not the tallest of lighthouses, but at 38-feet, it's high enough on the cliff that the light is able to flash out over the sea at 79-feet above water. The tower is owned by the Town of Bristol and is managed by the Bristol Parks Commission.

LEFT & ABOVE: Permaquid Point Light is famous for the strange, wave-like appearance of its rocks, produced by ancient glaciation and the action of the tides.

PORTLAND BREAKWATER LIGHT

Built: 1875
Style: Cast Iron
Height: 26 feet (7.92m)

Considered one of the "oddest" lights on the Atlantic Coast, this 33-foot tall light was erected to mark the end of the 2,000-foot breakwater and assist with guiding ships through the narrow entrance of Portland Harbor. Also known as "Bug Light," the beacon was designed intentionally as a replica of the Choragic Monument of Lysicrates in Athens.

In 1855 the site was established with an octagonal wooden light at the end of the breakwater. When the new light went up in 1875, it was built with six Corinthian columns around the perimeter of the light. It guided ships safely until 1942 when the light went dark. It wouldn't see activity again until 2002 when the South Portland Rotary Club and Spring Point Ledge Light Trust held a ceremony to show the public the refurbished the lighthouse.

Now operated and managed by the city of South Portland, the "Bug Light" sees thousands of visitors annually in what is now known as Bug Light Park. The light at the top of the short tower flashes white every four seconds.

HOW TO GET THERE

The lighthouse is not open to the public, but the grounds are open and it can be viewed up close. To get to Bug Light Park, take Broadway into South Portland. At the stop sign by the Spring Point Marina make a left, and then a right onto Madison Street. Look for the park signs and follow them to Bug Light Park. Free parking is available.

Address
South Portland Greenbelt Pathway
South Portland, ME 04106

RIGHT: The light was fully restored, reactivated, and then opened to the public in 2002. Today, the Bug Light Park allows visitors a closer view of the lighthouse, while also being a memorial to the shipbuilders of World War II.

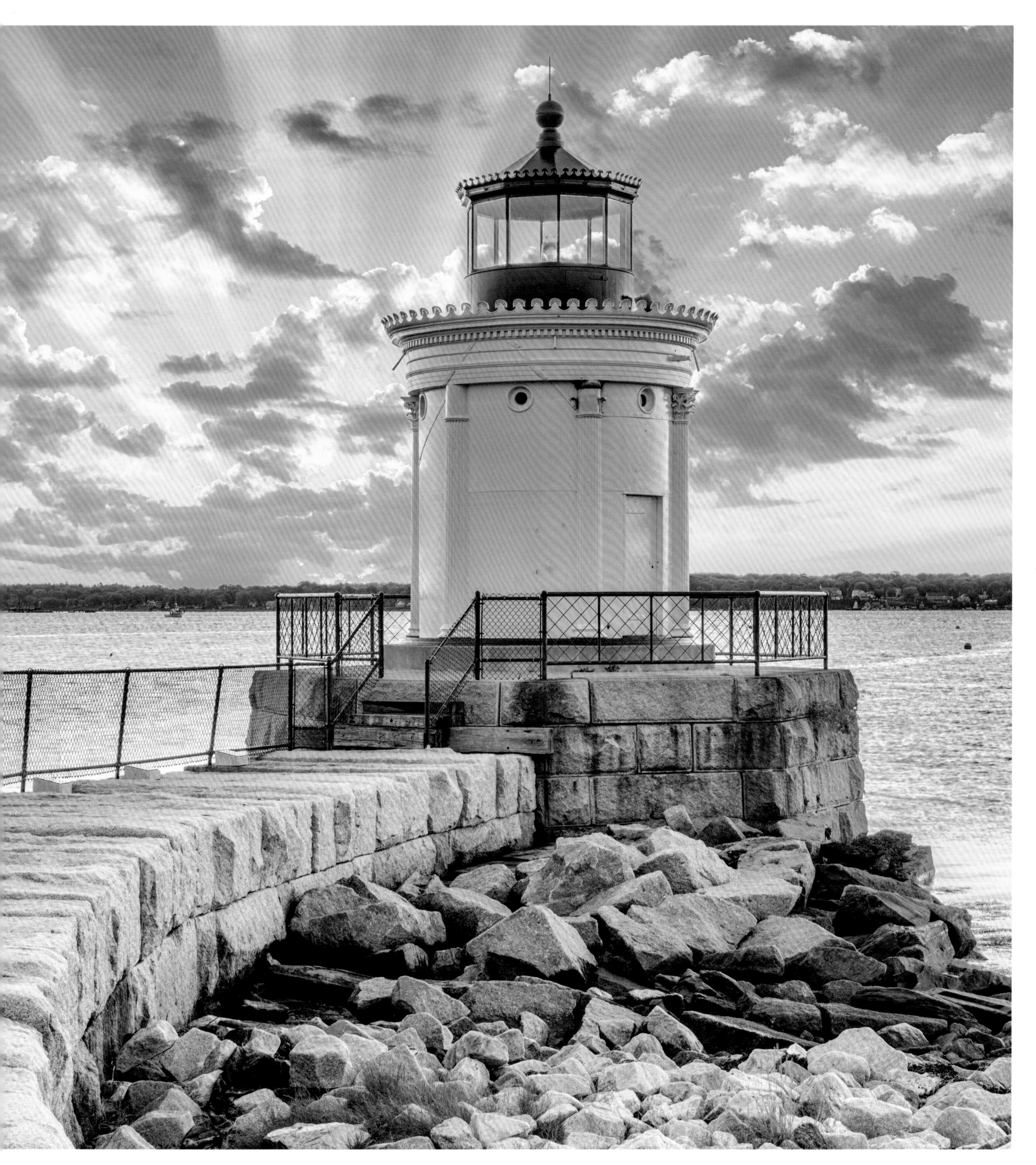

PORTLAND HEAD LIGHT

Built: 1791
Style: Conical Tower, Brick
Range: 24 miles (38.62km)
Height: 80 feet (24.38m)

Also known as the Cape Elizabeth Lighthouse, the Portland Head Light sits atop a rocky cliff at Casco Bay. The site was originally established in 1791 and is noted to be the first major lighthouse project tackled by the federal government in the late 18th century. It was the very first lighthouse built on the coast of Maine.

This iconic beam was the inspiration for Henry Wadsworth's poem, *The Lighthouse*. Since its inception, the landmark has undergone various transformations in height. In 1864, twenty feet were added to the tower and a Fresnel lens installed. But when the lighthouse at nearby Halfway Rock was erected, the significance of the Portland Light was downgraded and the tower shortened. Complaints from mariners changed that, however, and in 1885 the tower was restored to its original height.

During the rebuild in 1885, a spiral staircase was built inside. Preserved to near perfection, the lighthouse and the elaborate keeper's quarters are open to the public. The beautiful white house with its red roof has become iconic to the area. Originally built in 1891, the two-story dwelling kept keepers and their families safe during the worst storms. The US Coast Guard maintains the light and fog signal today, but the property is maintained by the Town of Cape Elizabeth. HORN

DAY MARKING - WHITE

RIGHT & INSET: The picturesque buildings of the Portland Head Light make favorite subjects for artists and photographers.

HOW TO GET THERE

Take 295 in Portland to Route 77 south directly into South Portland. Turn left on Broadway and then right onto Cottage Road. Cottage Road will eventually turn into Shore Road. There is no fee to enter the area, but donations to the Citizens of Cape Elizabeth are always appreciated.

Address
Fort Williams Park
1000 Shore Rd.
Cape Elizabeth, ME 04107

PORTSMOUTH HARBOR LIGHT

Built: 1878
Style: Cast Iron, Brick
Height: 48 feet (14.63m)

This distinguished light has been referenced by a few different names, including Fort William and Mary in its humble beginnings. Because money for public works was tight, colonial governments had to make do with what they had. That's why the first navigational light erected here in 1771 was merely a flagpole with a lantern hoisted to the top. It was eventually replaced by a hexagonal wooden tower. The tower was rebuilt after a small skirmish between soldiers unfolded on the site, and was aptly named Fort Constitution in 1804. Thirteen lamps lit the tower at the top to guide vessels on the water.

In 1851 the tower was shortened to 45-feet. Later, in 1871, the keeper's dwelling was torn down and replaced with a new one. The home was moved twice to make room for defensive walls. As modifications and changes continued on the site, the lighthouse was called Fort Point Light,

HOW TO GET THERE

The lighthouse is open to the public from May to October. There is no fee to climb the tower, but a donation is suggested. To get there take Plymouth Circle, Exit 5. Follow the signs for Hampton Beaches on Route 1 Bypass South. Continue on Route 1 Bypass South until the 6th traffic light. Here, turn left onto Route 1A, or Elwyn Road. There are two public lots available for parking.

Address
25 Wentworth Rd.
New Castle, NH 03854

New Castle Light, or Fort Constitution Light. Only a historian would remember it's original name of Fort William and Mary.

The first Fresnel lens used in the tower is still in active use today, illuminating a green light over the waters that is always on. While the light is managed by the US Coast Guard for navigation, the actual site is managed by the Friends of Portsmouth Harbor Lighthouses.

DAYMARKING—WHITE

LEFT & ABOVE: The Portsmouth Harbor Light has evolved from humble beginnings during colonial times to the tower seen here today. Dating from the mid 19th century, the present lighthouse has stood the test of time, and is still an active aid to navigation after more than 150 years of service.

ROCKLAND BREAKWATER LIGHT

Built: 1902
Style: House Style
Height: 25 feet (7.62m)

Rockland Breakwater light started its early years in 1888 as a "moving" light along a man-made stone breakwater extending from Jameson's Point. The breakwater was built to keep the harbor safe. But instead of making it safer, the extension actually became a hazard. This prompted workers to add a trapezoidal light at the end of the breakwater. It was a fixed white light that hung on an iron crane, some 24 feet above sea level.

BELOW & RIGHT: Rockland Breakwater Light sits atop a massive breakwater, built in 1888 to calm the waters in the harbor. Like many lighthouses today, the keeper's quarters now house a maritime museum.

DAYMARKING-RED BRICK

NOTE: ANTENNEA TV

With each extension of the wall, workers moved the trapezoidal light further and further out. It wasn't until 1902 that the square tower and the keeper's dwelling was constructed.

The Fresnel lens that once graced the top of the tower was removed and changed so the light could be automated in 1964. As it fell into disrepair, it was slated to be torn down in 1973. But public outcry halted the demolition. The City of Rockland now owns the refurbished light and keeper's house, and encourages visitors for a small donation. To get into the lantern room, visitors need to climb a 7-foot ladder for the very best view.

NOTE: SOLAR PANEL NO FLAG ON FLAGPOLE

HOW TO GET THERE

This iconic structure is open weekends in the summer. There is no fee to tour it, but a donation is suggested. To get to the lighthouse and back, walking along the ⅞-mile-long breakwater is necessary. You can get there by heading to West Penobscot Bay, which is on the south side of the entrance of Rockland Harbor. From US Route 1 in Rockland, turn onto Waldo Avenue. Then, make a right onto Samoset Road, which will take you directly into the parking lot of the lighthouse.

Address
West Penobscot Bay
Rockland, ME 04841

NOW TO GET THERE

The lighthouse is located on the east coast of Nantucket. The grounds are open to the public to view the lighthouse from the outside only. From Nantucket, follow Milestone Road. At Siasconset, bear left onto Sankaty Avenue. Turn right on Butterfly Lane, then left onto Baxter Road. The lighthouse is at the end of Baxter.

Address
Baxter Rd.
Nantucket, MA 02554

SANKATY HEAD LIGHT

Built: 1850
Style: Brick, Granite
Range: 24 miles (38km)
Height: 70 feet (21.33m)

Built on a 90-foot bluff, this lighthouse was the first in New England to have installed a Fresnel lens. Unlike some of the other lighthouses in North America, it burned so bright that mariners called it the "blazing star." The name Sankaty is said to come from the Native Americans, and means "cool hill." Local townsfolk used the high bluff as a lookout for whales on the hill that was known for its cool breezes.

The original cast iron lighthouse atop a brick dwelling was 53-feet tall. In 1884, iron stairs were built inside in the tower. In 1886, telegraph and telephone upgraded the lighthouse. That same year, a 50-foot pole was erected to display weather signals. A deck was also added, bringing the lighthouse to its current 70-feet.

In 1990, The Army Corp of Engineers believed the tower would tip over toward the eroding bluff within a decade. The keeper's house and other buildings were moved to avoid further erosion. One building was brought to town and used for housing. The other buildings were destroyed. After years of struggle with finding funding, an organization was formed to save the lighthouse. Today it sits 390 feet northwest from its original location on land donated by The Sankaty Head Golf Club. The light remains in active navigation, flashing every 7.5 seconds.

NIGHT MARKING
DAY MARKINGS: WHITE RED WHITE

LEFT: Today, the Sankaty Head Light stands as a sentinel for all who come to visit it. Visitors can also enjoy the wonderful setting atop the Sankaty Head bluff overlooking the Atlantic Ocean.

SAYBROOK BREAKWATER LIGHT

Built: 1838
Style: Brick, Cast Iron
Height: 50 feet (15.24m)

Also knows at the "Outer Light" by locals, this tower sits at the end of a stone jetty that extends into the Connecticut River, closely resembling a giant chess rook. It was the first lighthouse built to mark the mouth of the river at Long Island Sound. The tower was constructed as four floors, and included a basement and lantern room with twelve sides. A Fresnel lens was installed in 1886. A fog horn soon followed and was installed in 1899.

The tower is thick and solid and proved it wasn't going anywhere after a fierce hurricane tried to topple it in 1938. The bridge to the breakwater was torn away and two large tanks were swept into the water, too. Some windows were busted out and the basement flooded. But through it all, the tower remained up.

Today the light is privately owned by Frank Sciame, who bought it in an auction for $290,000 in 2015. Sciame once owned the property adjacent to the lighthouse and admired the tower from afar. The tower was purchased for renovations to become the family's summer home. It still aids in navigation today with a flashing green light.

HOW TO GET THERE

The lighthouse is closed to the public, but can be seen from various places along the shore. Take US Highway 1 into Old Saybrook. Turn onto US Route 154 toward Fenwick. The lighthouse can be seen from Route 154.

Address
Old Saybrook
(Viewed from) Route 154
Old Saybrook, CT 06475

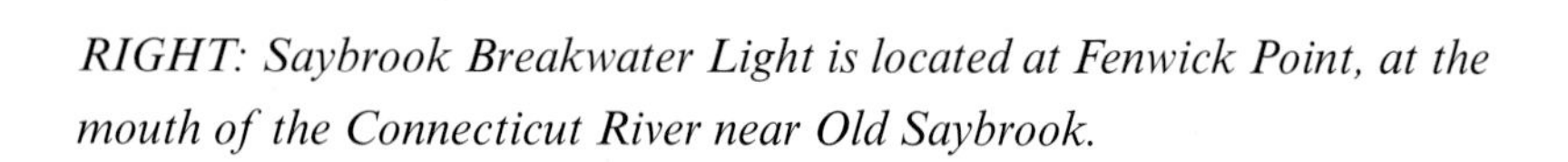

RIGHT: Saybrook Breakwater Light is located at Fenwick Point, at the mouth of the Connecticut River near Old Saybrook.

SANDY HOOK LIGHT

Built: 1764
Style: Octagon, Rubble Stone
Range: 19 miles (30.57km)
Height: 85 feet (25.9m)

Considered the oldest working lighthouse in the US, this New Jersey beacon at the mouth of the Hudson was often referred to as the "New York Lighthouse" in its early days. This is because its construction was paid for by New York merchants. After the revolution, a quiet civil war erupted between the two states over ownership.

Historians cite that a lighthouse was requested in the area as early as 1679. But it took three shipwrecks to happen in 1761 before the idea was fully entertained. It was erected and withstood the mighty winds and weather until 1857 when it underwent upgrades. This included a spiral iron staircase to replace the original wooden one.

The light has always been on in the lantern room, save it being darkened during the American Revolution and World War II. Early in the Revolutionary war, the British occupied the tower. Despite the soldiers attempt to bring it down with cannonballs, the tower stood strong, never allowing the artillery to damage it. The light was automated in 1962. Today the lighthouse still emits a brilliant, fixed white light over the Atlantic Ocean at Lower New York Bay.

DAY MARKING: WHITE
NIGHT MARKING: CONSTANT

HOW TO GET THERE

The lighthouse is open April through October. In Highlands, take Route 36 to Highlands Beach. Here, turn into Sandy Hook National Park. Follow the signs that will lead you to the lighthouse.

Address
85 Mercer Rd.
Highlands, NJ 07732

RIGHT: The Sandy Hook Light was designed and built by Isaac Conro in 1764. It was built to help mariners entering the southern end of New York harbor. Although it is in New Jersey, it was originally called the New York Lighthouse, because it was funded by a lottery and a tax on all ships entering the Port of New York.

SPRING POINT LEDGE LIGHT

Built: 1897
Style: Caisson-style, Brick and Cast Iron
Height: 54 feet (16.45m)

Sitting atop a breakwater near the entrance of Portland Harbor, this light is a caisson-style lighthouse. Caisson-style is also known as a "sparkplug" lighthouse and was developed as a more affordable means to erect a much-needed lighthouse on the water in the late 19th century. These kinds of lighthouses are offshore and often far more demanding, leaving lighthouse keepers secluded in their work. The circular catwalk around the structure is small, but as one lightkeeper noted, a mile could be achieved if he walked around it fifty-six times.

One of four lighthouses along the harbor, the light was built to warn mariners of a dangerous, submerged ledge. In the late 1800s, the area was recognized as one of the most traveled waterways for ships and schooners carrying much-needed food, coal, and other commodities. The breakwater there today was built in 1950 to connect the secluded lighthouse to the mainland. The light was automated in 1934 and is now overseen by the Portland Harbor Museum.

HOW TO GET THERE

The lighthouse is open to the public on weekends between Memorial Day and Labor Day. From downtown Portland, take Highway 77 over the Casco Bay Bridge. It will turn into Broadway. Take Broadway to the entrance of Spring Point Marina. Here, turn right on Benjamin W Pickett Street. Make a left onto Fort Road. At this point, drive through the campus of Southern Maine Community College to the parking area on the waterfront.

Address
Southern Maine Community College
Fort Rd.
South Portland, ME 04106

"She is like a revolving lighthouse; pitch darkness alternating with a dazzling brilliancy!"

Henry James

RIGHT: Spring Point Ledge Light was constructed in 1897 by the government after several steamship companies complained that many of their vessels ran aground on the submerged, Spring Point Ledge. Congress initially allocated $20,000 to the lighthouse's construction, although the total cost of the tower ended up being $45,000.

STATUE OF LIBERTY

Built: 1886
Style: Statue, Copper
Range: 24 miles (38.62km)
Height: 305 feet (92.96m)

Probably the most well-known tower and light throughout the world, the Statue of Liberty sits atop a massive granite pedestal in New York Harbor. Before it became a symbol for American freedom, it was an official lighthouse operated by the Lighthouse Board. It has welcomed millions of immigrants to the US since 1886.

The statue was a gift from France to honor the centennial anniversary of independence. The torch she holds was lit and became an operational lighthouse in November of 1886. She was also the first lighthouse to use electricity as its original source of power. Engineers struggled at first, however, and several attempts to light the torch failed. Eventually, their efforts paid off but it took nine electric arc lamps, plus five on the ground, to light the statue up. It takes visitors 354 steps to get to the top.

The torch was changed many times while it was in service, but the original light was eventually restored by the National Park Service in 1984. It can be viewed when you enter the lobby of the statue. In 1902, the light was decommissioned, based on reports that it was never considered a highly effective aid to navigation to begin with.

NIGHT MARKING - STEADY LIGH
DAY MARKING - GREEN COPPER

BELOW & RIGHT: The Statue of Liberty, a gift to the United States from the people of France, is a robed female figure representing Libertas, the Roman goddess of freedom, who bears a torch and a tabula ansata *(a tablet evoking the law) upon which is inscribed the date of the American Declaration of Independence. A broken chain lies at her feet.*

HOW TO GET THERE

There is a fee to enter the Statue of Liberty. From the east side of New York City, take FDR Drive south to Battery Park. Turn onto to State Street, or take the West Side Highway (9A) to Battery Place. Visitors will pay a fee to take the ferry over to the Statue of Liberty and Ellis Island.

Address
Battery Park
1 Battery Pl.
New York, NY 10004

WATCH HILL LIGHT

Built: 1855
Style: Square, Brick
Height: 51 feet (15.54m)

This prominent lighthouse is located on a peninsula in southeastern Rhode Island at the eastern entrance to Fishers Island Sound. The first tower established in the early 1800s was not to navigate ships, but to provide early warning of a naval attack during King George's War. The first time a lamp was raised to aid ships was in 1807 when a local carpenter constructed a round tower and fitted it with ten whale oil lamps.

In 1857, the Lighthouse Board saw fit to replace the existing tower with a 51-foot granite tower and attached house for the keeper. This lighthouse was fitted with a Fresnel lens with a fixed white light. It was

BELOW & RIGHT: A watchtower and a simple beacon were first established at Watch Hill by the Rhode Island colonial government in around 1745, giving the area its name. It may also have been used as an earlier lookout point by Narragansett Indians.

HOW TO GET THERE

The lighthouse is not open to the public, but can be accessed after a short walk from Larkin Road. Parking is available in the village of Watch Hill. The museum is open to the public on Tuesday, Wednesday, and Thursday afternoons. Take I-95 north to exit 92. Turn right onto CT-2. CT-2 becomes Liberty Street. Eventually merge onto CT-78E until it becomes Airport Road, which will eventually become Winnapaug Road. Make a left on Watch Hill Road, and then a left on Bluff Avenue. Bluff Avenue becomes Larkin Road. Turn left onto Lighthouse Road.

Address
14 Lighthouse Rd.
Westerly, RI 02891

later replaced with a flashing light so that navigators weren't confused by nearby streetlights.

The light was automated in 1986. Today the tower is managed by the Watch Hill Lighthouse Keepers Association. The US Coast Guard still uses the light as an aid to navigation.

DAY MARKING- GRAY TOWER
THREE WHITE
BLDG.
NIGHT MARKINGS- FLASHING

HOW TO GET THERE

The site is open to the public for tours. Located in Quoddy Head State Park, take ME-192 to Main Street, US-1 N. Take US-1 N to Lubec Road/ME-189. Turn right onto South Lubeck Road.

Address
973 South Lubec Rd.
Lubec, ME 04652

WEST QUODDY HEAD LIGHT

Built: 1858
Style: Brick, Cast Iron
Range: 18 miles (29km)
Height: 49 feet (14.93m)

The first tower built on this site was erected in 1808 by order of President Thomas Jefferson to assist in guiding ships through the Quoddy Narrows and is considered one of Maine's oldest light stations. The first keeper, Thomas Dexter, lit the wicks on the lamp for the first time in 1808. His pay of $250 a year wasn't enough to take care of he and his family, and so he pleaded to the government for more, citing that the soil on the property wasn't fair enough for planting. The government conceded and increased his pay to $300 a year.

The red and white candy-striped tower stands on the easternmost point of land in the United States. A foghorn, still in use, is housed in a separate, brick building. Technology allows the horn to go off thanks to sensors that can detect thick fog. Before the building was erected, cannons and bells were used to warn ships. The light is still used today, emitting two white flashes of light every 15 seconds.

Fifty steps on a spiral staircase take curious climbers up to the lantern room. The steps become steeper at the top where they reach a final 10-rung ladder. The visitor's center next to the lighthouse is managed by the Lightkeeper's Association and is non-profit making.

DAY MARKING RED + WHITE
CANDY STRIPE
NIGHTMARKING
FLASH
EVERY
15 SECS.

LEFT: The beacon and fog signal at West Quoddy Head have been in operation since 1908. Despite its relatively short tower, its light can be seen for up to 18 miles out at sea.

No Docking

LIGHTHOUSES OF THE SOUTHEAST

Dangerous shoals and reefs in the southeast area of the US forced Congress and the Lighthouse Board to take a closer look at the need for bright beacons along its shorelines. Some of the tallest and most enchanting lighthouses grace these shores, leaving behind stories of steadfastness during war, and legacies of brave captains and lightkeepers in their wake.

ASSATEAGUE LIGHT

Built: 1867
Style: Brick, Stone
Height: 142 feet (43.28m)

As commerce grew on along the Chesapeake Bay, shipwrecks were aplenty. Assateague was just one of many lighthouses along the southern coast that needed to be constructed in order to avoid more tragedies. The shoals there jutted out like sharp knives, and only a lighthouse could aid mariners in avoiding them.

The original lighthouse erected on the site was built in 1831 and was only 45-feet tall. It peeked above the trees just south of the Maryland border on Assateague Island, halfway between Chesapeake Bay and Delaware Bay. This first light was equipped with a Winslow Lewis lamp and reflectors but unfortunately, the light wasn't nearly as bright as it should have been. The Lighthouse Board had the tower and lamps torn down and appropriated funds for a new one. The Civil War would interrupt its progress until 1867. In October of that year, the massive tower was constructed and brightly lit with a Fresnel lens.

Assateague was automated in 1965 and is still used for navigation by the US Coast Guard today. The structure and property itself are maintained by the Chincoteague National Wildlife Refuge.

DAY MARKING - RED, WHITE, RED WHITE RED, WHITE, RED

BELOW & RIGHT: The Assateague Lighthouse is located at the southern end of Assateague Island off coast of the Virginia Eastern Shore. It is sited within the Chincoteague National Wildlife Refuge.

HOW TO GET THERE

The lighthouse is open to the public from April until November. There is no admission fee. Take US-13 on the eastern shore of Virginia to state 175 into Chincoteague. Follow signs to the Wildlife Refuge across the bridge to Assateague Island. Park in the lot and take the quarter-mile trail leading to the tower.

Address
Assateague Island National Seashore
Chincoteague National Wildlife Refuge
Chincoteague Island, VA 23336

BILOXI LIGHT

Built: 1848
Style: Brick, Cast Iron
Height: 61 feet (18.59m)

This tower on the Mississippi coastline has survived massive storms and the Civil War. As a result of its strength, locals say the landmark is a symbol of their own strength and resilience. The tower is bright white in color, but in 1865 after President Abraham Lincoln was shot and killed, the tower was temporarily painted black as a gesture of mourning.

In 2010, the lighthouse underwent extreme renovations at the cost of $400,000. It was rewired completely. The brink inside was also rebuilt. But most unique is the blue bands painted on the walls to show how high the water rose during hurricanes. It marks Hurricane Katrina in 2005 at 21.5 feet above sea level. In 1969, Hurricane Camille marked the walls at 17.5 feet. The cast iron shell and metal bars around the lantern room is credited for saving the light in countless storms, including the hurricanes.

Biloxi was the first cast-iron lighthouse built in the southern United States and is the second oldest in the country. Lightkeepers manned the tower from 1848 until 1939. Many female lightkeepers were responsible for maintaining the tower, including Maria Younghans. She manned the tower for over 50 years. The light is still a navigational aid to ships today. It shines using the original Fresnel lens.

BELOW & RIGHT: Built in 1848, the Biloxi Light was possibly the first cast-metal lighthouse to appear in the south. The light was operated by civilians from 1848 to 1939, and is notable for having several female lightkeepers, including Maria Younghans, who with her daughter tended the light for a total of 62 years. In 1939, the US Coast Guard assumed responsibility for the light's operation, and after being declared surplus to requirements in 1968.

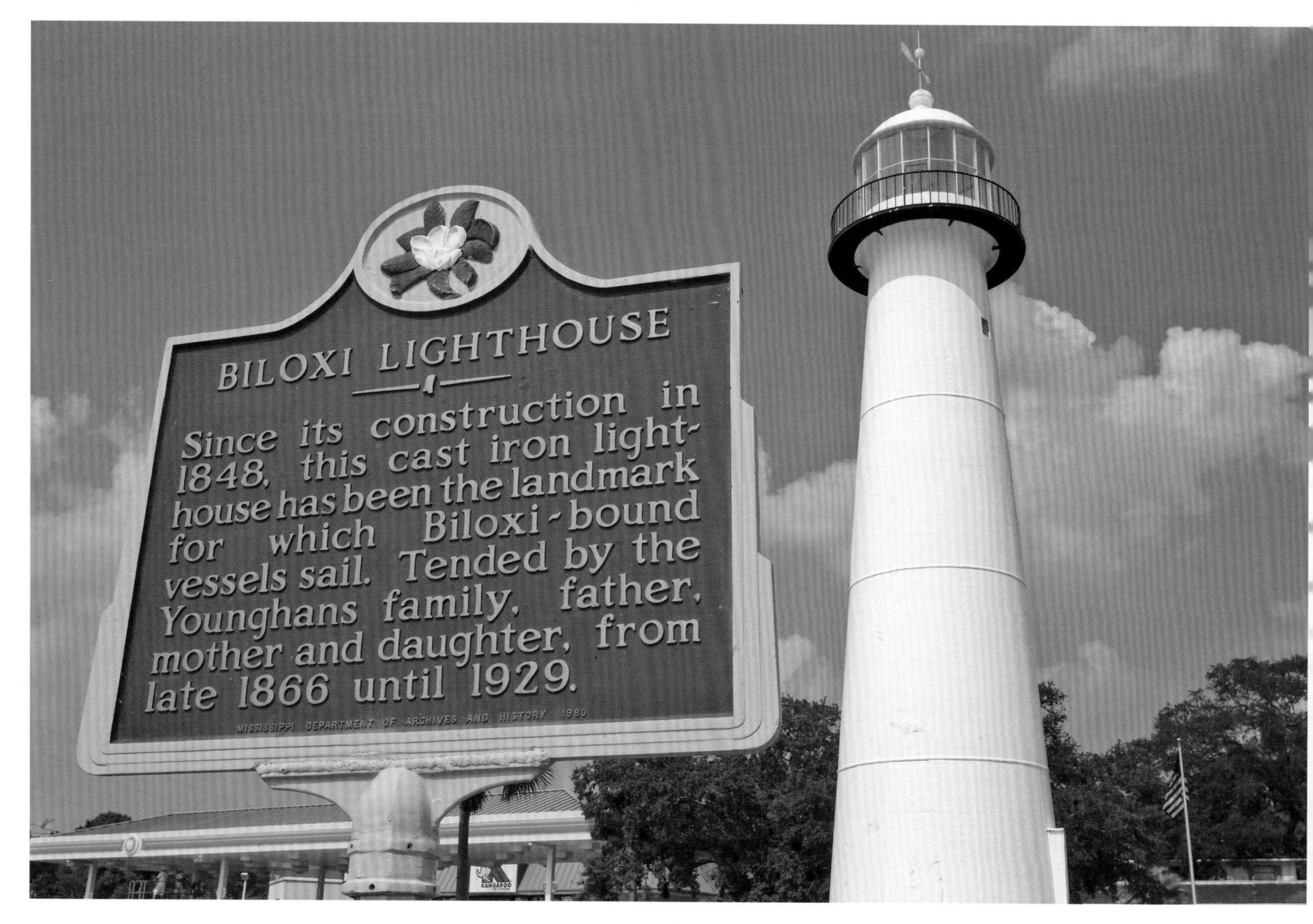

HOW TO GET THERE

Guided tours of the lighthouse for a small admission fee are available. Take US Highway 90 at Porter Avenue in Biloxi, just west of the I-100 loop and Beau Rivage Resort & Casino.

Address
Porter Ave.
Biloxi, MS 39530

CAPE FLORIDA LIGHT

Built: 1825
Style: Conical, Cast Iron and Brick
Height: 95 feet (28.95m)

Originally erected on Cape Florida thirty miles north of Carysfort Reef, the 65-foot light was constructed with walls five feet thick, or so it was thought. In 1836 Seminole Indians attacked the lighthouse, killing the assistant lightkeeper and setting the tower on fire. John Thomson, the lightkeeper, survived by hiding in the lantern room. For the next ten years, the tower would be unapproachable because the Indians settled there.

It wasn't until construction workers finally made their way to the tower in 1846 that they discovered the walls were actually hollow, and that the original builder had duped Congress.

Despite the repairs, it seemed the lighthouse still wasn't functioning at its best. Shipwreck after shipwreck was recorded, until it was determined that the tower wasn't tall enough for ships to see the lantern above. And so, in the 1850s, an additional 100 feet was added to the tower and a Fresnel lens installed.

All was well until 1861 when Confederate soldiers damaged the light, extinguishing it for a period of time. It was restored again in 1866, and even again after the Coast Guard refurbished the light and property in 1978. Visitors can take 112 steps to the top during a guided tour. Cape Florida Light is now owned and managed by the Florida Department of Environmental Protection.

BELOW & RIGHT: The Cape Florida Light marks the southeastern end of the Florida peninsula. Left to decay for over 100 years, it was returned to use in the 1990s.

HOW TO GET THERE

From Miami, take I-95 to the Rickenbacker Causeway until you reach Bill Baggs State Cape Florida State Park. The park is at the southern end of Key Biscayne.

Address
Bill Baggs State Cape Florida State Park
1200 S. Crandon Boulevard
Key Biscayne, FL 33149

CAPE HATTERAS LIGHT

Built: 1870
Style: Conical, Brick
Range: 20 miles (32.18km)
Height: 193 feet (58.82m)

HOW TO GET THERE

The lighthouse is open to the public and offers private tours and self-guided tours. There is a fee to climb the tower. To get there, head to the Village of Buxton on Cape Hatteras National Park Road until it turns into NC-12/NC Highway 12. Turn left onto Forest Road. Forest Road will turn into Lighthouse Road.

Address
46379 Lighthouse Rd.
Buxton, NC 27920

The first lighthouse to grace this site was erected in 1803. It stood 95 feet tall and was made of sandstone. At the top, wicks burned off whale oil to light the waters below. Located on the Outer Banks, this North Carolina light is part of the Cape Hatteras National Seashore. But, as was the case with many early lighthouses, it wasn't tall enough, nor was the light strong enough. It was eventually rebuilt to what it is now.

The current conical brick tower was constructed after the Civil War when a Navy inspector called it "the worst light in the world." It was painted with black and white spiral stripes. Also known as a daymark, the stripes were put there to help the tower stand out during the daytime.

By the early 1990s the tower, battered with erosion, was quickly falling apart. To save it and the surrounding structures, each building had to be moved 2,900 feet inland. It took 23 days to move all of the structures, including the lighthouse. Today, it is well preserved and awaits eager visitors to take all 248 spiral steps to the top.

DAYMARK- BLACK & WHITE
SPIRAL STRIPES

RIGHT: The Cape Hatteras Light, was moved to a safer location inland, due to the erosion of the shoreline. Pictured here is after it had been moved to its new, safer location.

CAPE LOOKOUT LIGHT

Built: 1859
Style: Conical, Brick
Range: 19 miles (30.57km)
Height: 163 feet (49.69m)

Located on the southern Outer Banks of North Carolina, the original light at Cape Lookout had the same story as some of its neighbors: the light was too weak and the tower too short. A bright beacon on this shoreline was necessary, especially considering the nickname mariners gave the area was "Horrible Headland."

Improvements to the light were made in 1859 and a Fresnel lens was placed in the lantern room. But it barely led ships in before the light succumbed to the tragedies of war. During the Civil War, troops at nearby Fort Macon shot out the lens.

The lens was repaired and the light was lit again until it became automated in 1967. Today the lantern boasts an updated beacon that flashes every 15 seconds. Visitors can expect a 207 step climb to the top, which is the equivalent of walking up a 12-story building.

DAYMARKING - BLACK & WHITE DIAMONDS
NIGHTMARKINGS - FLASHES ONCE EVERY 15 SECONDS

HOW TO GET THERE

The lighthouse can only be accessed by taking a ferry. The Island Express Ferry Service is authorized to take visitors to the lighthouse. To get to the ferry service, take US-70 E to West New Bern Road. Continue until it becomes US 70 E again. Turn right onto Turner Street. Make a left onto Front Street. Reservations for the ferry are recommended in advance.

Address
Island Express Ferry Service
600 Front Street
Beaufort, NC 28516

LEFT: The lighthouse is part of the Cape Lookout National Seashore and can only be accessed by private ferry. A few times a year, visitors are allowed to climb the 207 spiral iron steps to the top of the lighthouse.

CAPE SAN BLAS LIGHT

Built: 1885
Style: Iron, Skeletal
Height: 98 feet (29.87m)

If there was ever a lighthouse that fell on hard times, it would be the Cape Sans Blas Light. It has been rebuilt, refurbished, and redesigned at least four times. When it was first constructed in 1847 it lasted only four years before a hurricane tore it down. Contractors rebuilt it with brick in 1856. But it didn't survive. Once again, a hurricane tore it down.

A third tower was built in 1859. But as was the case with many southern towers, it suffered the wrath of war. Confederate forces blasted out the Fresnel lens and torched the tower. Understanding the need to continue to light the waterway here, the Lighthouse Board allocated funds to rebuild the damaged lighthouse in 1882. But the ship carrying the materials to build it sunk. Not ready to give up, they decided to build the next tower with iron, and, in 1885, the current iron tower was erected.

To prevent it from being damaged during storms, it was constructed so that it could be disassembled prior to a hurricane. This approach clearly worked, as the tower still stands proudly today on the shores of St. Joseph bay where it was moved to save it from coastal erosion and preserve the iconic structure. The move was made in 2014.

BELOW & RIGHT: Cape San Blas Light was plagued by disasters from the very first, including hurricanes, disease, and war. The present lighthouse, the fifth in a chain dating back to 1847, was built in 1885, and although it was moved in 2014, its tower still stands.

HOW TO GET THERE

Take I-95 S and I-10 W to Gadsden County. From there, take exit 174 from I-10 W. Follow FL-12 W and FL-71 S to Harborview Drive in Port Saint Joe.

Address
George Core Park
Port St. Joe, FL 32456

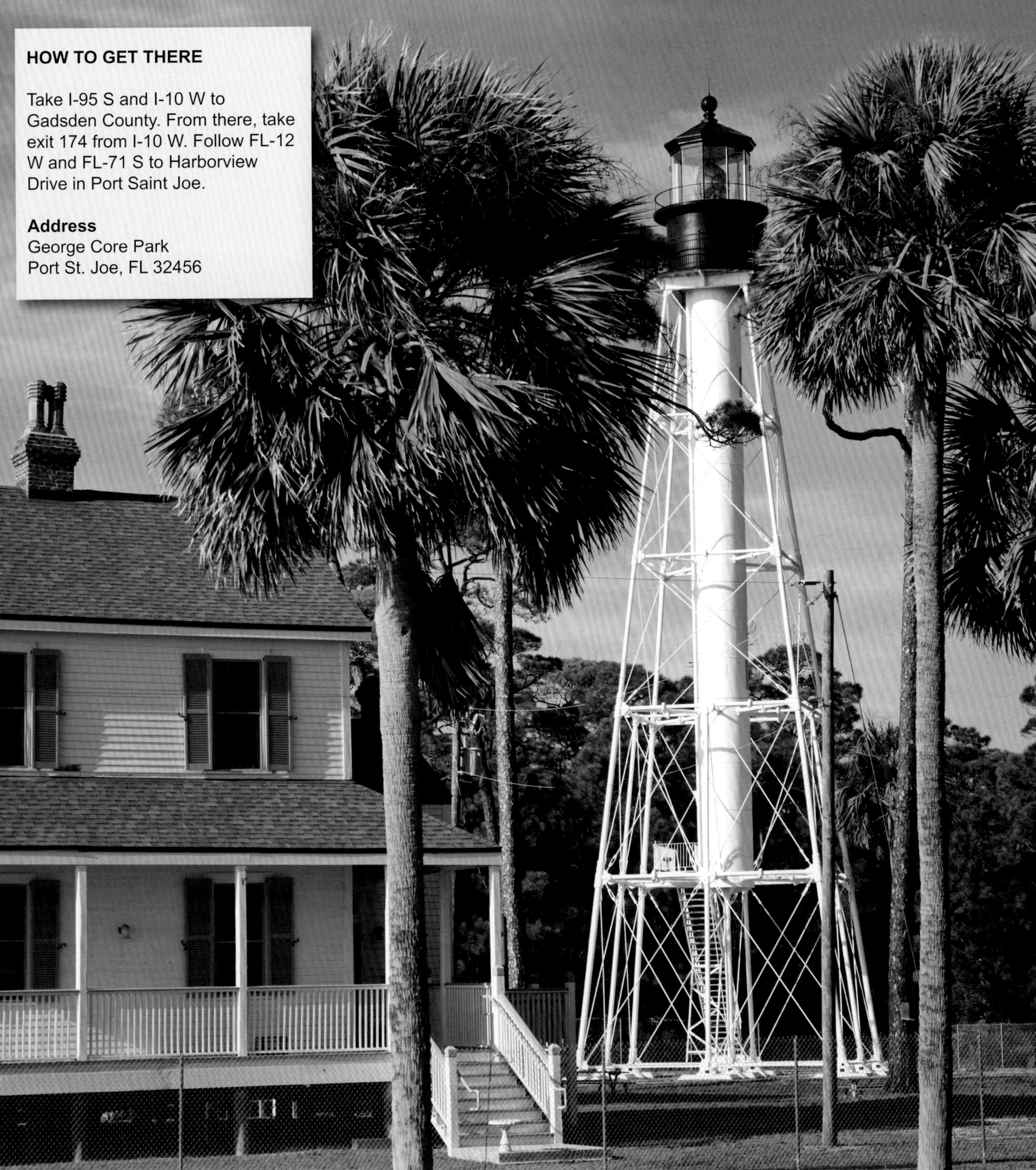

COCKSPUR ISLAND LIGHT

HOW TO GET THERE

The light is closed to the public as restorations efforts continue, but the iconic tower can be viewed from afar. To see it, take Route US-80 from Savanna. The tower can be seen from the US-80 bridge.

Address
US-80
Savannah, GA 31410

Built: 1849
Style: Brick
Height: 48 feet (14.63m)

Also known as the South Channel Light, this tower was built with its companion light, the North Channel light. The duo of towers guided ships on the Savannah River near Tybee Island until the North Channel Light on Oyster Island was destroyed during the Civil War. Cockspur, or the South Channel, survived the artillery.

This tower is infamous for a love story. It is said that Florence Martus, the sister of a lightkeeper, met a handsome sailor who promised to return and marry her. As his ship departed, she stood in front of her cottage, waving a white handkerchief. She continued to wave the white linen at every passing ship for the next 50 years. While her sailor never returned, the story of her loyalty spread to mariners everywhere. Many would send her gifts from distant ports to help ease her heart.

After the war was over the tower was relit and continued to serve the channel until it went dark in 1949. The park service assumed control and refurbished the light, but it has since fallen in great disrepair. Efforts to obtain a restoration grant of $1.4 million dollars are underway.

"And it was a most remarkable, a most moving glance, as if for a moment a lighthouse had looked at me."

Ford Madox Ford

LEFT: The National Park Service is dedicated to the preservation of this lighthouse. It is currently closed to the public while restoration work is carried out.

CONCORD POINT LIGHT

Built: 1827
Style: Granite
Height: 30 feet (9.14m)

The Concord Point Light is the oldest lighthouse in Maryland, proudly built with local Port Deposit granite. The walls of the tower are three feet thick. The original light at the top was a lantern that illuminated the waters with a set of lamps surrounding sixteen-inch reflectors. It was later replaced with a small Fresnel lens.

The lighthouse keepers at this location are unique in that they all came from the O'Neil family. The first was John O'Neil, who is said to have stood up against an entire British fleet to protect the lighthouse. Somehow he survived and was awarded the job of keeper immediately following. Every successor thereafter was a relative until the 1920's when the light was eventually automated. It was decommissioned in 1975.

Today the light is still used as a navigational aid. Visitors can take twenty-seven granite steps to the top for a breathtaking view.

BELOW & RIGHT: The Concord Point Light is located at the point where the Susquehanna River meets the tidal flow of Chesapeake Bay. Here, the waters are hazardous to navigate.

HOW TO GET THERE

The lighthouse is open April to October on weekends. Admission is free, but donations are welcome. To get there, take State Route 155 to 1-95 and make a left onto Otsego Street. Turn right onto Saint John's Street, and then a left at the Concord Point sign. The light is near the Susquehanna River in the southeast part of town.

Address
700 Concord St.
Havre de Grace, MD 21078

CURRITUCK BEACH LIGHT

Built: 1874
Style: Conical, Brick
Range: 19 miles (30.57km)
Height: 158 feet (48.15m)

Standing tall above the trees at the border of the North Carolina and Virginia coasts, this mighty red brick tower was constructed with one million bricks in 1874. Strategically placed between the Cape Hatteras Lights and Bodie Island Lights, this lighthouse illuminated one of the last remaining stretches of the southern coastline. A "stick-style" keeper's dwelling was built on site in 1876. Two families lived there, sharing the two-family home in an isolated area, as they tended regularly to the tower.

The massive lighthouse has successfully survived powerful Atlantic storms. While most towers are painted with daymarks or solid colors, this tower was left in its original state so that it wouldn't be confused with the others. It was automated in 1939. The light still flashes today at 20-second intervals to help guide vessels safely along the coastline.

BELOW & RIGHT: The Carrituck Beach Light was built to fill the "dark spot," that existed between the light at Cape Henry, Virginia and that at Bodie Island. Like other lighthouses on North Carolina's Outer Banks, the Carrituck Beach Light still serves as an aid to navigation.

HOW TO GET THERE

The lighthouse is available for tours from Memorial Day to Labor Day. There is a small fee to climb. To get to the tower from Kitty Hawk, head north off of US-158. This is also the Outer Banks Highway. Turn onto NC 12 and head twenty miles into the Village of Corolla. The lighthouse can be seen on the left.

Address
1101 Corolla Village Rd.
Corolla, NC 27927

DRUM POINT LIGHT

Built: 1883
Style: Screw-pile, Cottage-type
Height: 46 feet (14.02m)

The current location of this iconic lighthouse is not its original location. Moved in 1975 to preserve it, the light is now part of the Calvert Maritime Museum. Prior to the move, this unusual looking lighthouse was located at the entrance of Maryland's Patuxent River and served the Chesapeake Bay in the early 20th century. Fitted with a Fresnel lens, it emitted a fixed red light to warn ships of the sandy spit off of the point. The hexagonal part of the structure was made of wood, while the screw-pile base was wrought iron.

The light was strongly anchored in ten feet of water, roughly 100 feet from shore. But as tidal patterns shifted, the light eventually stood above water in low tide. By the 1960s, the US Coast Guard no longer saw the need for the light and decommissioned it. It was moved to the museum in the mid-70s and has since been preserved to the likeness of the light and how it may have looked in the early 1900s.

HOW TO GET THERE

The museum and lighthouse are open to the public for an admission fee. To get there, take Route 4 from Washington, D.C., to Solomons. The museum and lighthouse can be found near the bridge across the Patuxent River.

Address
4275 Solomons Island Rd. S.
Solomons, MD 20688

THESE PAGES: Drum Point Light was decommissioned in 1962. It was moved up the Patuxent River to the Calvert Marine Museum at Solomons in March 1975, where, with advice from the daughter of the last keeper, it was restored to its former glory.

DRY TORTUGAS LIGHT
or Loggerhead Lighthouse

Built: 1858
Style: Brick
Range: 20 miles (32.18km)
Height: 157 feet (47.85m)

In the early 19th century, a weak navigational light constructed on Garden Key was said to be responsible for the demise of the ship, *America*. After years of controversy regarding the poor functionality of the light, funding was allocated to construct a second light station on Dry Tortugas.

Dry Tortugas is a seventy-square mile cluster of shoals, reefs, and islands. Once considered one of the most dangerous waterways in the Gulf of Mexico, the black and white tower has withstood numerous hurricanes since it was constructed. The hurricane of 1873 attempted to take it down, but workers made fast repairs to salvage what damage did occur. Their repairs were so well done, that no other hurricane has threatened the tower since.

The light was automated in 1987 and is still used as a navigational aid under the watchful eye of the US Coast Guard. This lighthouse is often referred to as the Loggerhead Lighthouse.

"Anything for the quick life, as the man said when he took the situation at the lighthouse."

Charles Dickens

HOW TO GET THERE

The lighthouse is located in Dry Tortugas National Park. The only way to view the tower is via ferry. To get to Yankee Fleet Ferry in Key West, Take US-1 toward Key West. Turn right onto North Roosevelt Boulevard (US-1 S/FL-5), then make a right onto Palm Avenue. Palm Avenue becomes Eaton Street. Make a right onto Margaret Street.

Address
Yankee Fleet Ferry
240 Margaret St.
Key West, FL 33040

RIGHT: Located on Loggerhead Key, the Dry Tortugas Light was constructed in 1858 as a result of the numerous issues with the Garden Key Light. The light was taller, brighter, and equipped with a more modern optical lens than the Garden Key Light.

GARDEN KEY LIGHT

Built: 1876
Style: Cast Iron
Height: 37 feet (11.27m)

Known as the light responsible for the demise of the America, the first Garden Key light in Fort Jefferson was made of brick and stood sixty-five feet tall. It was erected in 1823. It was a crucial light that was built to help guide vessels coming from the Mississippi River with raw materials. During the years the Garden Key light was active, so was the fort that surrounded it. While the fort never saw battle, it did become a prison and housed some 900 inmates, including four men convicted of taking part in the assassination of President Abraham Lincoln.

Not long after the inmates were pardoned, a second lighthouse, the Dry Tortugas Light, was built after complaints of Garden Key being a poor navigational aid were finally addressed. But the Garden Key Light wouldn't stand for long. In 1873 a hurricane damaged it so badly, it had to be torn down. It was rebuilt as the cast iron tower that sits atop the walls of the fort today.

HOW TO GET THERE

Like the Dry Tortugas Light on the previous page, the Garden Key Light is also located in Dry Tortugas National Park. The only way to view the tower is via ferry. To get to Yankee Fleet Ferry in Key West, Take US-1 toward Key West. Turn right onto North Roosevelt Boulevard (US-1 S/FL-5), then make a right onto Palm Avenue. Palm Avenue becomes Eaton Street. Make a right onto Margaret Street.

Address
Yankee Fleet Ferry
240 Margaret St.
Key West, FL 33040

ABOVE: The Garden Key Light stands on ruins of Fort Jefferson, a historical military fortress in Dry Tortugas National Park.

RIGHT: This lighthouse was one of three lighthouses to be commissioned for construction in the Florida Straits in 1824 by the United States Congress.

GEORGETOWN LIGHT

Built: 1812
Style: Conical, Brick
Height: 87 feet (26.51m)

The original lighthouse erected on this site was made of cypress and stood seventy-two feet tall. The tower was built for $7,000 on land donated by a Revolutionary War patriot by the name of Paul Trapier. Next to the light was a small keeper's dwelling and a storage building that held vats of whale oil for the wicks of the lamps.

In 1867 Confederates used the tower as a lookout station, taking 124 steps to the top to scope out the enemy. During battle, the tower was badly damaged and needed to be reconstructed. Postwar repair work included heightening the tower and adding a brighter Fresnel lens.

Today the Georgetown Light is noted as being the oldest operating lighthouse in South Carolina. The property there was once owned by former Boston Red Sox owner, Tom Yawkey. In his will, he offered all but the lighthouse to the South Carolina Heritage Preserve.

HOW TO GET THERE

The lighthouse is located 14 miles from the port city on North. It is closed to the general public but can be viewed from a ferry. Rover boat tours take visitors past the iconic tower. Call 843-546-8822 for tour information.

Address
Winyah Bay
North Island
Georgetown, SC 29440

"Guide-star of hope, whose bright translucent ray
Directs the sailor on the devious way;
Warns him of craggy rocks, of quicksands drear,
And forms a light his fragile bark to steer."

John William Smith

RIGHT: The Georgetown light is situated on North Island at the entrance to Winyah Bay, southeast of Georgetown. It is maintained by the US Coast Guard.

HARBOUR TOWN LIGHT

Built: 1970
Style: Octagonal, Stucco
Height: 90 feet (27.43m)

The Harbour Town Light may be one of the newest lights built in North America. It is unique in that it wasn't built as a navigational aid, but constructed instead to attract tourists on Hilton Head Island. Visitors climb 110 stairs to the top where they can look out over the marina below. There is also a gift shop at the top.

Built under the direction of developer Charles Fraser, some believed the light would be ineffective and called the light "Fraser's Folly." But by the 1980s, the lighthouse, painted red and white, became the island's trademark.

The lighthouse frames the 18th hole of the Harbour Town Golf Links and is the backdrop for one of golf's most picturesque finishing holes. Despite its original purpose, the light is found on navigational maps. The light in the lantern room blinks every 2.5 seconds.

LEFT & RIGHT: The Harbour Town Lighthouse is a tourist attraction on Hilton Head Island. The privately owned lighthouse also features a museum dedicated to Harbour Town and gift shops. It is the first privately financed lighthouse to be built since the early 1800s.

HOW TO GET THERE

The lighthouse is open to the public for an admission fee. To get there, take US-278 E. Make a left onto Cross Island Parkway. After the toll, the Parkway becomes Palmetto Bay Road. Make a right onto Greenwood Drive.

Address
Sea Pines
175 Greenwood Dr.
Hilton Head Island, SC 29928

HILLSBORO INLET LIGHT

Built: 1906
Style: Octagonal, Skeletal
Range: 25 miles (40.23km)
Height: 137 feet (41.75m)

The Hillsboro Inlet lighthouse has a timeline different than most in that it took a period of seven years to fund it, build it, and light it. What's more, it wasn't built on site, but constructed by a Chicago company and then shipped down the Mississippi to be viewed first at the St. Louis Exposition. When the government realized there was a functioning lighthouse that could be utilized as an actual navigation light, it was loaded onboard giant vessels again, and delivered to the northern side of Miami where it sits today.

The massive structure was anchored into the ground by six huge iron piles, a design considered to hold up against common hurricane weather. The anchoring worked. Lighthouse keepers here needed to be fit and lean. They were required to climb 175 steps several times a day with buckets of kerosene to fuel the lamps. The lens was rotated by early mechanical clockwork controlled by a weight that had to be raised every half hour.

The daymarks of the skeletal structure are black and white, and were painted this way to distinguish Hillsboro Inlet from neighboring Juniper Inlet and Cape Florida. The name of the tower comes from the Earl of Hillsboro, who was the surveyor of many parts of Florida in the 1700s.

LEFT & RIGHT: The Hillsboro Inlet Light is at 137 feet one of the tallest of Florida's iron-skeleton towers. It was originally built in Chicago, where it featured in the 1904 St. Louis Exposition. It was dismantled and reassembled at Pompano Beach a few years later.

HOW TO GET THERE

A small boat ride from Alsdorf dock takes visitors to the lighthouse for a fee. To get to the northside of Alsdorf Park, take I-95 to 14th Street causeway. Head east to just before the bridge. The park is on the north side of the road.

Address
2974 N.E. 14th St.
Pompano Beach, FL 33062

HOOPER ISLAND LIGHT

Built: 1902
Style: Caisson, Cast Iron
Height: 63 feet (19.20m)

Deemed Chesapeake Bay's youngest light, this off-shore light was built to warn ships of the dangerous shoals between Smith Point and Cover Point. It sits boldly in eighteen feet of water, leaving lighthouse keepers of the day isolated for long periods of time in the four-level cast iron tower.

The two bottom floors were originally made of hardwood, while the top two floors of the lighthouse were made of cast iron. This includes the watchroom, which houses a curved ladder that allows keeper's access to the lantern room via a small trap door. The lighthouse was also originally equipped with a Fresnel lens, which flashed in the lantern room every fifteen seconds. In 1961 the light was automated. For fifteen years the automated light blinked without the aid of a keeper until 1976 when the massive Fresnel lens was stolen. The US Coast Guard replaced it with an updated solar light at that time.

Today the lighthouse still sits quietly in the water, waiting for a steward to take care of it. The US Coast Guard still uses it as an aid for navigation, but now seeks a non-profit organization that can maintain the structure and perhaps open it to the public.

HOW TO GET THERE

The lighthouse is closed to the public but can be seen from Hooper Island and via a boat tour from Sawyer Fishing Charters. To get to the marina, take MD-335 and turn right onto Hoopers Island Road, and then make a left onto Hoopersville Road.

Address
Sawyer Fishing Charters &
Chesapeake Bay Tours
747 Hoopersville Rd.
Fishing Creek, MD 21634

RIGHT: The Hooper Island Light is located in Chesapeake Bay, west of Middle Hooper Island in Maryland. It was added to the National Register of Historic Places in December 2002 and officially turned over to the US Lighthouse Society in June 2009.

HUNTING ISLAND LIGHT

Built: 1875
Style: Cast Iron
Height: 136 feet (41.45m)

This massive white and black lighthouse stands 136 feet tall inside a short, white fenced-in area, and is the only lighthouse in South Carolina currently open to the public. Not unlike many of its neighbors, this light met battle during the Civil War and plunged into darkness for a short time. Congress thought the Confederates toppled it completely, although others believe erosion dropped it into the water. The tower remained a pile of ruins until 1875 when the Lighthouse Board commissioned funds to have it rebuilt as a cast iron tower that could be disassembled and moved, if necessary.

In 1889 the lighthouse did, indeed, need to be moved. Thanks to beach erosion it was relocated 1¼ miles inland. Visitors can take 167 steps to the top to take in a view of the Atlantic Ocean. The light is no longer in service, but the tower still offers a fascinating history to its visitors.

BELOW: The incredible view looking northeast from Hunting Island Light.

RIGHT: The Hunting Island Light has a reputation for being haunted.

HOW TO GET THERE

There is a fee to tour the lighthouse. To get there, take US-17 N/Trask Parkway toward Exit 33, the Point South exit. Then take US-21 east from Beaufort to Huntington Island State Park.

Address
Huntington Island State Park
2555 Sea Island Parkway
St. Helena Island, SC 29920

JUPITER INLET LIGHT

Built: 1860
Style: Iron
Height: 125 feet (38.1m)

LEFT & BELOW: The impressive Jupiter Inlet Light, built before the Civil War, has survived the ravages of time, war, and natural phenomena to function as an effective beacon to this day.

HOW TO GET THERE

The bright red lighthouse can be seen from the US-1 bridge over Jupiter Inlet, north of West Palm Beach. Take I-95 (exit 87A) to Indiantown Road East and turn left on US Highway 1. Make a right at onto Beach Road, and then another right onto Lighthouse Park. Follow the road to the parking lot and museum. There is a fee to climb the tower.

Address
500 Captain Armour's Way
Jupiter, FL 33469

Dubbed the Jewel of Jupiter, this historic site was originally surveyed by Robert E. Lee. And if ever there was a light that should be noted for the amount of manual labor it took to build it, it is this one. Building materials for the Jupiter Inlet Light were transported thirty-five miles by ship. To get the 500 tons of materials that were needed to erect the tower, the trip had to be made fifty times. By July of 1860, the tower was finished and ready to illuminate the water for the first time.

The island was quite isolated. When lighthouse keeper Captain James A. Armour arrived to mend the light hidden in a nearby creek (he would stay there as keeper for the next forty years), he brought his wife with him. There wasn't another female around for at least 100 miles.

The light would be extinguished in 1928 after a hurricane took it out. The second keeper, Charles Seabrook, was forced to reinstall the original mineral lamps to keep ships from colliding on the waters below. When he fell ill from the hard work, his 16-year-old son successfully completed the job.

KEY WEST LIGHT

Built: 1848
Style: Conical, Brick
Height: 65 feet (19.81m)

When the US Navy recognized the need for a lighthouse in Key West harbor as early as 1823, it was so they could safely oversee the arrival of military and commercial ships. And while that makes the tower notable, what makes it even more interesting is that the very first lighthouse keeper here was a woman.

Keeper Michael Mabrity was the first to light and man the tower, but his wife, Barbara, did much of the work to keep the lighthouse functioning and in good order. When her husband contracted yellow fever a few years later, she took over all duties completely, while still raising her six children. In 1846, the tower was toppled by a hurricane. Barbara Mabrity survived, but some of her children did not.

A new tower, the one currently on site, was constructed in 1848. This tower was also manned by Barbara Mabrity. Ten years later, a Fresnel lens arrived and was installed. It is the very light still used today. Barbara was relieved of her duties at the ripe age of eighty-two. Her granddaughter and daughter, with their respective husbands, assumed the position at the light following her death.

BELOW & RIGHT: Key West Light and its associated buildings now serve as the Key West Lighthouse Museum.

HOW TO GET THERE

Take Florida Turnpike South and merge into FL-821 toward Homestead. Then take US-1 toward Key West. Turn right onto Roosevelt Boulevard/US-1S/FL-5/. Continue until you see Whitehead Street and turn right. Parking is available.

Address
938 Whitehead St.
Key West, Florida 33040

CAPE HENRY LIGHTS

OLD CAPE HENRY LIGHT (short)
Built: 1792
Style: Sandstone, Brick
Height: 90 feet (27.43m)

NEW CAPE HENRY LIGHT (tall)
Built: 1881
Style: Cast Iron
Height: 350 feet (106.68m)

While this pair of lighthouses look very different, they are both similar in that the construction of each tower was delayed for different reasons. The Old Cape Henry Light at the entrance of Chesapeake Bay was delayed because of the American Revolution and was stalled for eighteen years because of it. The New Cape Henry Light went through a series of unfortunate construction mishaps, not the least of which was when one builder tried to salvage stones placed there for the tower twenty years earlier. The stones had sunk into the ground and could not be dug out.

When the first sandstone light was finally built, it was deemed unfit for use after standing for eighty years. The Lighthouse Board waited for it to crumble into the sea as they constructed its black and white neighbor, but the shorter sandstone tower never did. In the meantime, they build the iron tower 100 yards to the southeast, never expecting the sandstone tower, now with massive cracks in it, to sustain.

Since then, the lighthouse has undergone massive reconstruction. It is the fourth oldest lighthouse still standing in the United States. Both lighthouses are located on Fort Story in the city of Virginia Beach. Fort Story is a military base operated by the US Navy. Only the sandstone (Old Cape Henry) is open to the public. The taller, checkerboard lighthouse is still used for navigation today and is not currently open for tours.

LEFT, ABOVE & RIGHT: Both lighthouses have been placed on the US National Register of Historic Places and are designated as National Historic Landmarks.

HOW TO GET THERE

Located on Fort Story at the north end of Virginia Beach. To reach the fort, take US-60 from Norfolk and exit toward Va Beach/Little Creek. Turn left onto Shore Drive/US-60E. Continue for about 13 miles until 6th Street. Turn left on 6th Street, and then make a right onto Atlantic Avenue.

Address
Fort Story
583 Atlantic Ave.
Fort Story, VA 23459

OCRACOKE ISLAND LIGHT

Built: 1823
Style: Conical, Brick
Height: 64 feet (19.5m)

The first tower of this name was erected in 1803 on Shell Castle Island where it is said the British found and killed the pirate Blackbeard in the early 18th century. Shortly thereafter, lightning struck the tower and took it down.

The existing tower was rebuilt near Ocracoke Village is the oldest lighthouse in North Carolina, making it the second oldest in all of the United States. While it's the smallest of the towers on the Outer Banks, it served its purpose along one of the busiest shipping ports on the coast of North Carolina as it navigated ships and vessels through the Ocracoke Inlet.

The small tower is only eighty-six steps to the top where a Fresnel lens still brightens the way for boats on the water. The original light was removed by Confederate troops during the Civil War so they could use the short stack as a watch tower, but it was put back and relit by Union forces in 1864. Visitors can't climb the tower, but they can still view the beauty of the iconic structure, as well as visit the museum.

ABOVE & RIGHT: The Ocracoke Island Light. The Ocracoke Island was first put on the map when English explorer Sir Walter Raleigh touched land here in the late 1500s.

HOW TO GET THERE

The tower is accessible by ferry to Ocracoke Island. If you take the Swan Quarter Ferry, it will drop you near NC-12. Take NC-12 to Irvin Garrish Highway and turn right. Turn left to stay on the Irvin Garrish Highway. Make your first right onto Lighthouse Road.

Address
360 Lighthouse Rd.
Ocracoke, NC 27960

PONCE de LEON INLET LIGHT

Built: 1887
Style: Conical, Brick
Range: 17 miles (27km)
Height: 168 feet (51.20m)

This massive tower is the second tallest of all American lighthouses and was originally known as Mosquito Inlet. The Lighthouse Board deemed a light along the 60-mile stretch between St. Augustine and Cape Canaveral necessary as early as the 1870s, but work wasn't completed until 1887. Records show that a lighthouse was constructed here in 1835, but it was taken down by a storm before it was ever lit. This was not the case with the second, current lighthouse. A Fresnel lens with five wicks provided the light on the waters below.

In 1970, the Coast Guard discontinued the light, using a steel tower constructed at Smyrna Dunes Coast Guard station instead. But when nearby high-rise construction blocked the new, steel tower, eyes went back to the tall and mighty Ponce de Leon Inlet light, and it was recommissioned in 1983.

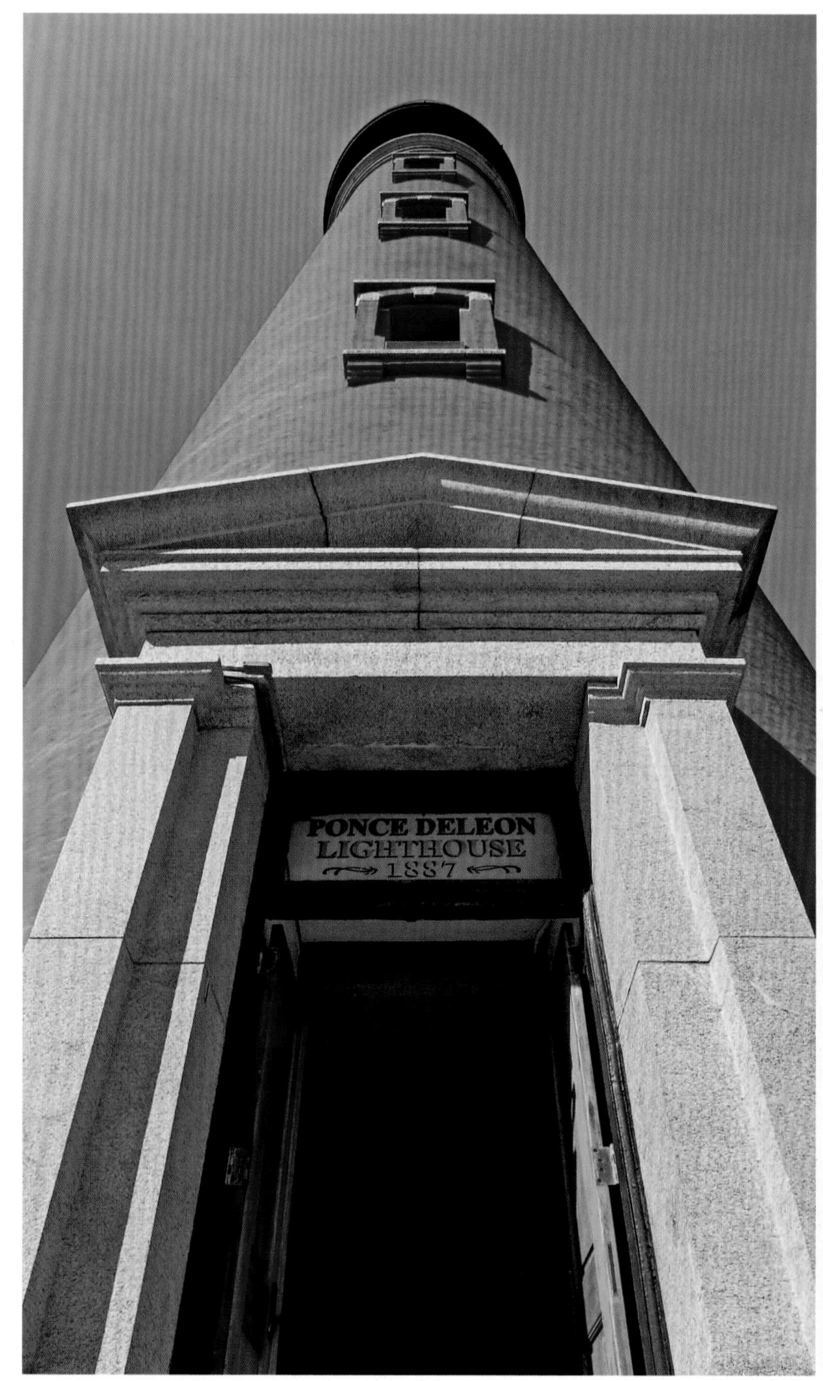

"It is during our darkest moments that we must focus to see the light."

Aristotle

THESE PAGES: In 1983 the light was restored to active service, primarily because high-rise buildings blocked the Coast Guard's beacon on the other side of the inlet. The lighthouse and three keepers' dwellings have been restored, and are open to the public.

HOW TO GET THERE

The lighthouse and the grounds surrounding it are open Memorial Day through Labor Day for an admission fee. From the beach on South Atlantic Avenue (A1A), head south toward Dunlawton Avenue. Continue to Beach Street in Ponce Inlet and make a right. Turn left onto South Peninsula Drive, and then a left into the lighthouse parking lot.

Address
931 South Peninsula Dr.
Ponce Inlet, FL 32127

SEVEN FOOT KNOLL LIGHT

Built: 1855
Style: Screw-pile
Height: 39 feet (11.88m)

The last screw-pile tower in all of Chesapeake Bay, this massive round structure was built to mark a dangerous shoal at the entrance of Baltimore Harbor. It sat atop eight iron piles in muddy water with a Fresnel lens at the top. Lighthouse keepers lived in the one-story cylindrical dwelling, but for some, it wasn't the best of living conditions. In the early 20th century it was reported that it was difficult to keep lighthouse keepers on site because of the "uncomfortable conditions in the station during the winter months." Other families reported that they didn't mind the round living quarters and made the best of it by bringing in a piano and plenty of books for entertainment during the cold spells.

The construction of this lighthouse was unique in that it was one of the first to use prefabricated parts. The walls and some beams were put together in Baltimore at the iron foundry and shipped to Chesapeake Bay to be assembled. The light was automated in 1948 and eventually abandoned by the Coast Guard in 1969. The City of Baltimore adopted the light as a museum, and the 220-ton structure was moved via barge to Pier 5 in the Inner Harbor district.

BELOW & RIGHT: The Seven Foot Knoll Light originally stood in open water at the entrance to the Patapsco River, Chesapeake Bay. In 1988, the lighthouse was moved to Baltimore's Inner Harbor, where it is now part of the Baltimore Maritime Museum.

HOW TO GET THERE

The lighthouse can be toured by the public and is located on Pier 5 of Baltimore's Inner Harbor next to the Baltimore Aquarium. Take I-83S to exit 23A toward Baltimore. Then take Exit 1, Fayette Street. Turn right onto Fayette Street. Make a left onto Saint Paul Street. The first right is East Baltimore Street.

Address
201 E Baltimore St.
Baltimore, MD 21202

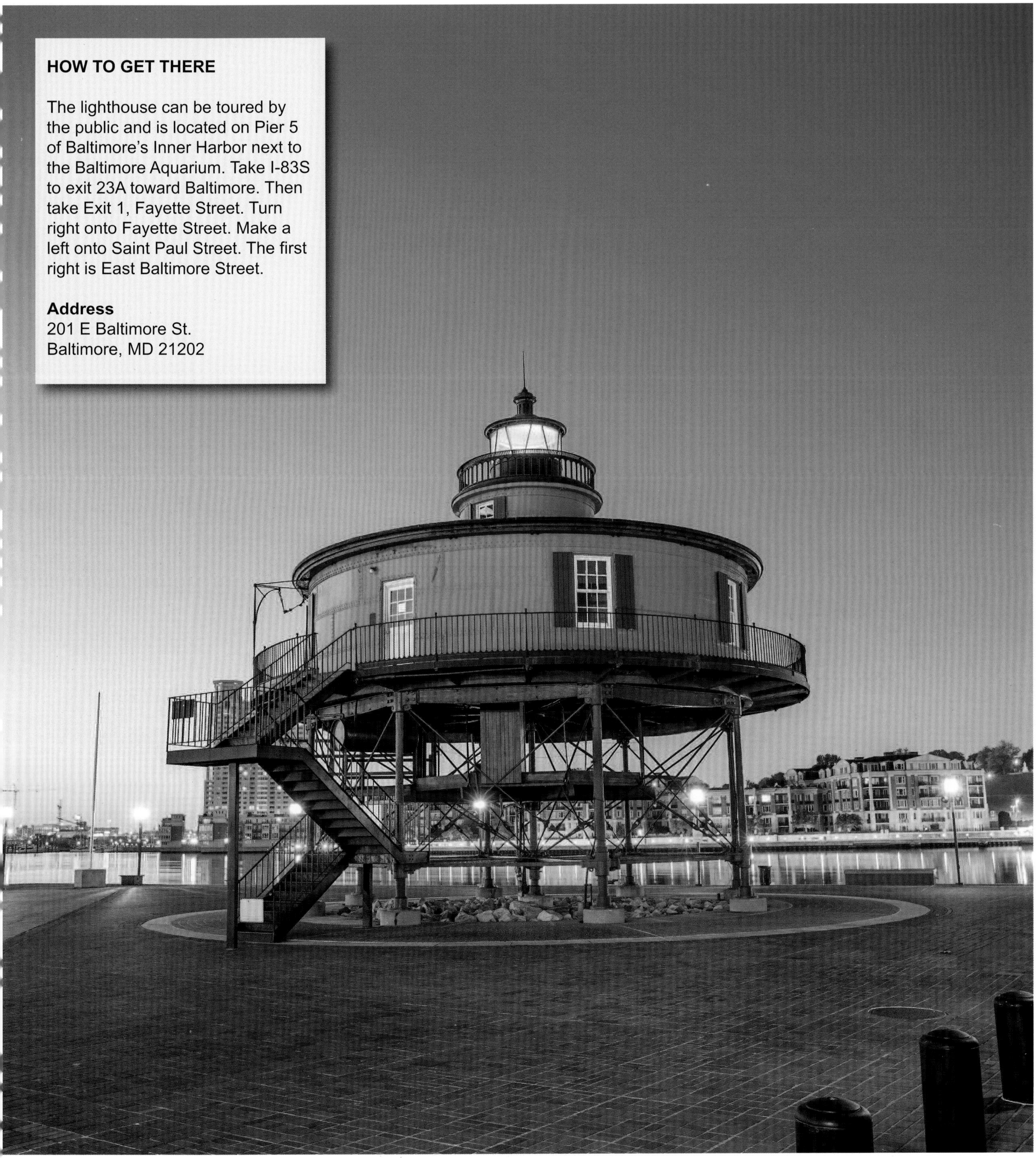

SOMBRERO KEY LIGHT

Built:1858
Style: Skeletal, Cast Iron
Height: 142 feet (43.28m)

This tall, skeletal tower was one of the more expensive towers to construct, costing the government a whopping $150,000 dollars. For 1858, that was a hefty price tag. But the cost has paid off over and over again, as the enormous tower has never toppled during even the worst of storms. It did, however, trap some of the lightkeepers during a 1926 hurricane.

Despite radios in the tower, no one could be reached. Keepers logged winds whipping in at 125 miles per hour. When the storm was over, the keepers assessed the damage, only to find that part of the tower's landing platform was washed away. The ladders to the platform were completely destroyed. But the massive structure itself remained unharmed.

Built by George Meade, a contractor who would later become a Union commander in Gettysburg, built the tower atop galvanized steel pilings in the water. The lighthouse was equipped with a bright Fresnel lens, which was replaced in 1984 with a modern optical light. However, the light was deactivated in 2015. A nearby 30-foot tower has since replaced the navigational purposes of the Sombrero Key Light.

HOW TO GET THERE

The light is not open for tours, but can be viewed from Sombrero Beach Park or mile marker 50 off of US-1. In Marathon, take US-1 to Route 931/Sombrero Key Road. Continue along Sombrero Key Road for two miles to the parking lot.

Address
Sombrero Beach
Sombrero Key Rd.
Marathon, FL 33050

RIGHT: The Sombrero Key Light is the tallest lighthouse in the Florida Keys. It was one of the first galvanized-steel constructions and took four years to build.

ST. AUGUSTINE LIGHT

Built: 1874
Style: Conical, Brick
Range: 25 miles (40.23km)
Height: 165 feet (50.29m)

Not long after the United States acquired Florida from the Spanish in 1819, a customs agent constructed the first primitive lighthouse by placing a lantern in an old stone tower to help guide mariners toward St. Augustine. The structure was eventually replaced by a 73-foot tower. But the weak light on the new tower proved useless. Nonetheless, the tower stood untouched until it met its demise during the Civil War. This time soldiers weren't to blame. Tidal erosion took the structure down.

Government officials allocated funds to build a new tower on nearby Anastasia Island. A high-quality Fresnel lens was installed and the light was lit for the first time on October 15, 1874. The light was set to flash some 25 miles through the darkness. Donned with a Daymark of black and white barber pole stripes, this iconic structure still houses and uses its original Fresnel lens. Visitors can take 219 steps to the top for a breathtaking view.

ABOVE: View of the Matanzas River and bay from the top of the St. Augustine Light.

LEFT & RIGHT: St. Augustine's present light was completed in 1874, having replaced two previous structures. The building was considered modern for its time. The lighthouse is now maintained as a private aid to nagivation and also houses a museum.

HOW TO GET THERE

There is a fee to see the lighthouse and related museum. To get there, take Philips Hwy/US-1 S/FL-5 to West Castillo Drive and make a left. Stay on West Castillo Drive until it becomes South Castillo Dr/FL-A1A. Continue to follow FL-A1A. Make a left onto Cathedral Pl/FL-A1A. Continue to follow FL-A1A. Turn left onto White Street East, and then a right onto Lighthouse Avenue.

Address
81 Lighthouse Ave.
St. Augustine, FL 32080

HOW TO GET THERE

The lighthouse is not yet open to the public but can be viewed from a distance. To see it, take Route 363 from Tallahassee to the St. Marks National Wildlife Refuge. Turn onto CR-59, and then onto Lighthouse Road.

Address
St. Marks National Wildlife Refuge
1255 Lighthouse Rd.
St. Marks, FL 32355

ST. MARKS LIGHT

Built: 1867
Style: Conical Brick
Range: 20 miles (32.18km)
Height: 82 feet (25m)

Third time's a charm for the St. Marks lighthouse on the shore of the Gulf of Mexico. Originally constructed in 1831, the lighthouse was so poorly built, it was ordered to be torn down by the Lighthouse Board. A second was rebuilt that same year, but met the fate of shoreline erosion in 1840, and was relocated. The tower was eventually met by gunfire during the Civil War and was badly damaged.

The current tower was constructed atop a 12-foot deep limestone foundation. It is the second oldest light station in Florida. The original light was made of fifteen lamps with fifteen-inch reflectors. One of the lightkeepers feared for his life during the Civil War, as many Seminole Indians were taking over Florida towers. But luckily, the Indians skipped this particular light. However, rebel soldiers did not. They blasted the lighthouse, nearly toppling it over. While it suffered damage, it managed to balance itself on the rubble until it was reconstructed in 1867.

The lighthouse is no longer in use, but is well-preserved thanks to the Florida Lighthouse Association. It sits quietly inside St. Marks National Wildlife Refuge. Donations are being collected to fully renovate the tower and the keeper's dwelling. A $550,000 grant was allocated in 2016 by the government for the renovations.

LEFT: The heavily fortified St. Marks Light, completed in 1867, was the fourth such lighthouse to be built on this vulnerable site. Fortunately, it has been able to survive its predecessors.

HOW TO GET THERE

Visitors can see the lighthouse for a fee. From downtown Savannah, take I-16 E to Martin Luther King Junior Boulevard and get off at exit 167A. Turn left onto Martin Luther King Jr Boulevard. Make a right onto West Bay Street. Next, merge onto US-80 E/Islands Expressway. Continue on US-80 E. Make a left onto North Campbell Avenue. Make another left onto Van Horne Avenue. Turn right onto Meddin Drive.

Address
30 Meddin Dr.
Tybee Island, GA 31328

TYBEE ISLAND LIGHT

Built: 1867
Style: Conical, Metal
Range: 20 miles (32.18km)
Height: 154 feet (46.93m)

Georgia's oldest and tallest light, the history of this beacon goes all the way back to 1733, when a wooden tower with a raised lamp was constructed on Tybee Island. It was built by James Oglethorpe, the founder of the colony of Georgia.

Erected at the entrance of the Savannah River, the first tower was destroyed by storms and rebuilt in 1791. But this second tower wouldn't last long. Fire took it the same year, leaving the island empty of a lighthouse until another was rebuilt in 1861, this time with brick. And, as was the fate of many towers of the day, the lighthouse was compromised by Confederate soldiers who burned it to the ground shortly after it was erected. The wooden stairs were completely gone, too, leaving the damaged light helpless at the top.

After the war, the structure was rebuilt as the 154-foot tower on site today. Massive brick walls at the base of the tower were put there to protect any future siege. In 1867, a Fresnel lens was placed in the lantern room and is still used today. The daymark on the tower is black and white, and is comfortably gated behind a white fence. The lighthouse made its debut with the US postal service in 2003 when it was featured on a commemorative US postage stamp.

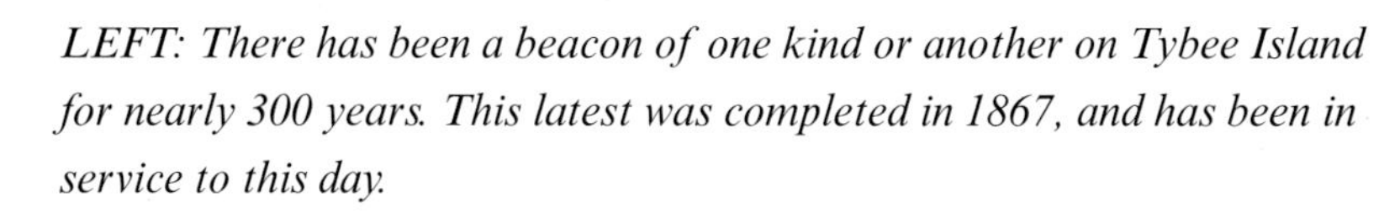

LEFT: There has been a beacon of one kind or another on Tybee Island for nearly 300 years. This latest was completed in 1867, and has been in service to this day.

FORBES ISLAND
FORBES ISLAND

LIGHTHOUSES OF THE WEST

Lighthouse lovers who explore the beaches or hike the bluffs of the West Coast can take in a breathtaking view of some of the most iconic beacons built along the Pacific Ocean. The whipping winds coming off the water fill the senses with the salty sights, smells, and sounds of the seas. Discover the shorelines that mariners navigated to avoid large rocks and other shipping hazards using one of seventy lighthouses built along the waters in the 19th and 20th centuries. Many have since crumbled and are no longer in existence, but thanks to historians and various non-profits, several lighthouses still stand strong on the Pacific Coast.

ALCATRAZ ISLAND LIGHT

Built: 1909
Style: Octagonal, Concrete
Height: 84 feet (25.6m)

Before the prison and before the lighthouse, the Island of Alcatraz was known as the Island of the Pelicans. It was made infamous after the Alcatraz Federal Penitentiary was built. Mobsters like Al Capone were housed there. The prison was supposed to be "inescapable" because of its high concrete walls and shark-infested waters surrounding it. But in 1962, three men changed that perception. Clarence Anglin, his brother John Anglin, and Frank Morris escaped Alcatraz and allegedly drowned in San Francisco Bay. Only recently has a claim come out that John Anglin, now in his 80s, is still alive.

Next to the cold walls of the prison stands the 84-foot lighthouse, a beacon of hope for mariners navigating the waters of the San Francisco Bay. The original tower, the first ever to be built on the Pacific Coast, fell prey to the great San Francisco earthquake of 1906. The damaged tower was replaced by the current structure and included a bay-style dwelling for the lighthouse keeper. A Fresnel lens was placed in the lantern room.

For several years lighthouse keepers endured the noise and turbulence of neighboring prison during riots. Their days were interrupted and sleep lost when the inmates wreaked havoc. In 1946 two prisoners took over the penitentiary for two days. During the takeover, the keeper and the lighthouse remained unharmed. The last keeper said good-bye to the dangerous post when the light was automated in 1963. The keeper's dwelling remained untouched until a demonstration of Native Americans burned it to the ground in 1969. Today the lighthouse is still a navigational aid, a white flash of light blinking over the waters every five seconds. The Golden Gate National Recreation Area oversees the maintenance of the lighthouse.

HOW TO GET THERE

The only way to visit the island is via ferry and take a guided tour with Alcatraz Cruises from Pier 33 Alcatraz Landing. To get to the pier, take Highway 101N towards the Bay Bridge. Exit at 4th Street. Merge onto Bryant Street. Follow Bryant Street to The Embarcadero. Make a left onto The Embarcadero. Continue for just under two miles to the pier. Parking is available.

Address
Pier 33, The Embarcadero
San Francisco, CA 94133

RIGHT & INSET: Today, the lighthouse is preserved as part of the Golden Gate Recreational Area, and like the old prison, is open to the public.

HOW TO GET THERE

The lighthouse is open to the public for no fee Memorial Day through Labor Day. To get there, take I-5 S via EXIT 2B toward Tacoma/Portland. From here, Take EXIT 163A toward W Seattle Bridge N/Columbian Way/W Seattle Bridge. Stay on the bridge until the Admiral Way exit. Continue on SW Admiral Way. Make a right onto 63rd Avenue SW. Next turn left onto Alki Avenue SW.

Address
3201 Alki Ave. SW.
Seattle, WA 98116

ALKI POINT LIGHT

Built: 1913
Style: Octagonal
Height: 37 feet (11.27m)

When the first lighthouse on this site was established, it was because the landowner recognized the need to illuminate the wedge-shaped point so that mariners could safely navigate around it, and therefore hung a small lantern as a humanitarian gesture. At the time, the waterway wasn't used much for shipping purposes. Because of this, landowners called the thrust of land "Alki," meaning "by-and-by."

While nearby Seattle continued to bustle with commerce, the southern entrance to Seattle's Elliott Bay did not. However, as Tacoma grew, things began to change and the waterways between Seattle and Tacoma became more populated. In 1887 the lighthouse board recognized this and funded the installation of a small lantern and lens on site.

As more ships passed in the night, the need for a stronger, brighter light was communicated. In 1913, that need was heard and the board purchased the land and built a stable lighthouse with an attached fog-signal structure and two keepers' dwellings, both with eight-rooms. The light itself was dressed with the popular and widely-used Fresnel lens, which burned with kerosene. The last lightkeeper retired his post in 1970. Shortly thereafter, the valuable lens was stolen. No leads ever tracked police to the thief. A short time later, a woman approached police after her husband bought the light from an antique dealer. Remarkably, the thief's fingerprints were still present on the light, and he was convicted. A new optic light is on the tower today and is still used as an aid to navigation by the US Coast Guard. The Alki Point Light is one of thirteen lighthouses still left along the shores of Puget Sound.

LEFT & INSET: Alki Point Light station is in the hands of the US Coast Guard. Tours are periodically offered by the US Coast Guard Auxiliary.

BATTERY POINT (CRESCENT CITY) LIGHT

Built: 1856
Style: Cape Cod
Height: 45 feet (13.71m)

This remarkable light sits atop a cape-cod style dwelling on the rocky cliffs of Battery Point. It was a much-needed beacon, considering the damage the sharp rocks could do to the vessels passing by below. In the 1850s, the Lighthouse Board recognized that Crescent City was a site that badly needed illumination so that freighters could safely guide massive loads of redwood bound for San Francisco. In 1856 it was constructed, fully equipped with a Fresnel lens.

The first keepers assumed their duties and kept the light lit over the harbor. In 1875, Captain John Jeffery assumed the post and stayed there for the next three decades. Here he raised his four children. During harsh weather, the family stayed safe behind the thick brick walls of the home. Still in its original form today, the house even withstood the tremors of the 1964 earthquake that struck Alaska. The resulting waves that were forced to shore somehow spared the dwelling, and both the house and the light atop it remained unharmed. The tsunami was one of the worst ever to hit the West Coast.

Today, the lighthouse is open to the public, but only during low tides. This is because sneaker waves can pop up at any time, putting visitors in danger. The care of the lighthouse is under the watchful eye of the Del Norte County Historical Society.

BELOW & RIGHT: Battery Point was built to guide shipping into the small lumber town of Crescent City.

HOW TO GET THERE

Visitors can get to the lighthouse by merging onto US-199 S via exit 55 toward Redwood Highway/Ocean Beaches/Crescent City. From here, merge onto US-101 S. Make a right onto Front Street and then a left onto Lighthouse Way. A half a mile up is the intersection of Battery Street and A Street.

Address
Battery St. and A St.
Crescent City, CA 95531

CAPE BLANCO LIGHT

Built: 1870
Style: Conical, Brick
Height: 95 feet (28.95m)

This solid white structure stands a total of 245 feet above sea level, warning ships and vessels to beware the white cliffs that drop almost vertically toward the beach on the southern Oregon coast. Cape Blanco is the oldest operating light station in this heavily foggy area and has guided many a ship to safety. Its remote location, however, proved challenging for lighthouse keepers. Strong winds kept them on their feet, but the weather eventually defeated them during a high-wind storm in 1878, ripping part of the roof of the dwelling. Shutters were later put over the windows to prevent them from being shattered in future wind storms. Keepers worked hard at their post, often walking supplies from the beach to the house before a road was built in 1885. It was hard, physical labor, but the keepers knew what to expect and stood up to the challenge.

Built to last with a brilliant Fresnel lens, the lighthouse fell prey to vandalism in 1992 when the antique light was smashed with a crowbar. This would typically be the end of a light with so many pieces and prisms, but an optician in a nearby town was able to salvage it. After seeking out matching pieces of glasswork, he was able to reverse-engineer the creation of the light by reinventing antiquated equipment that would have made the original glass pieces. After painfully executing the process, he was able to rebuild five of the damaged prisms. Thanks to his dedication and talent, the rebuilt lens still operates in the lighthouse today.

THESE PAGES: Cape Blanco Light is a great place to visit, with lots to do in the area including hiking and camping.

HOW TO GET THERE

Located in Cape Blanco State Park, the lighthouse is open for tours from April until October for a fee. To get there, take Highway 101 about five miles north of Port Orford. Head west to Cape Blanco Road, and then follow the road past the historic Hughes House to the very end.

Address
91100 Cape Blanco Rd.
Port Orford, OR 97465

CAPE MEARES LIGHT

Built: 1890
Style: Octagonal, Iron
Height: 38 feet (11.58m)

Sometimes placement of these iconic lighthouses isn't always accurate. Originally intended for Cape Lookout, the Cape Meares lighthouse station ended up on Cape Meares after a mapmaker made an error. Somehow the name got switched with another lighthouse on the US Coast Survey charts but went unnoticed until the lighthouse was almost complete. Despite the error, the Lighthouse Board decided to leave the light where it was. Once a Fresnel lens was placed inside, it turned out that the location worked after all, and mariners trusted this guiding light for years.

One of the first to sail into Tillamook Bay was Captain John Meares. He noted the area was often muddy at low tide and gave the bay the nickname of Quick Sand Bay. It didn't stick, but his name did. While it is the shortest lighthouse in Oregon, it proved to be quite effective. Five wicks kept the oil lamp bright with a large reflector to help illuminate it. The light was rotated by a 200-pound weight that had to be manipulated by the hands of the keeper. He turned it every two and a half hours.

Today, the light is fully automated and still acts as a navigational aid. It's not in the lighthouse, however, but in a building adjacent to it on the site. After the light was deactivated in 1963, the property was vandalized more than once. Since then, Friends of the Cape Meares Lighthouse have worked to restore the property and it is now open to visitors.

BELOW & RIGHT: Built in 1890, Cape Meares Light complex included two keepers' houses, two oil houses, and two cisterns.

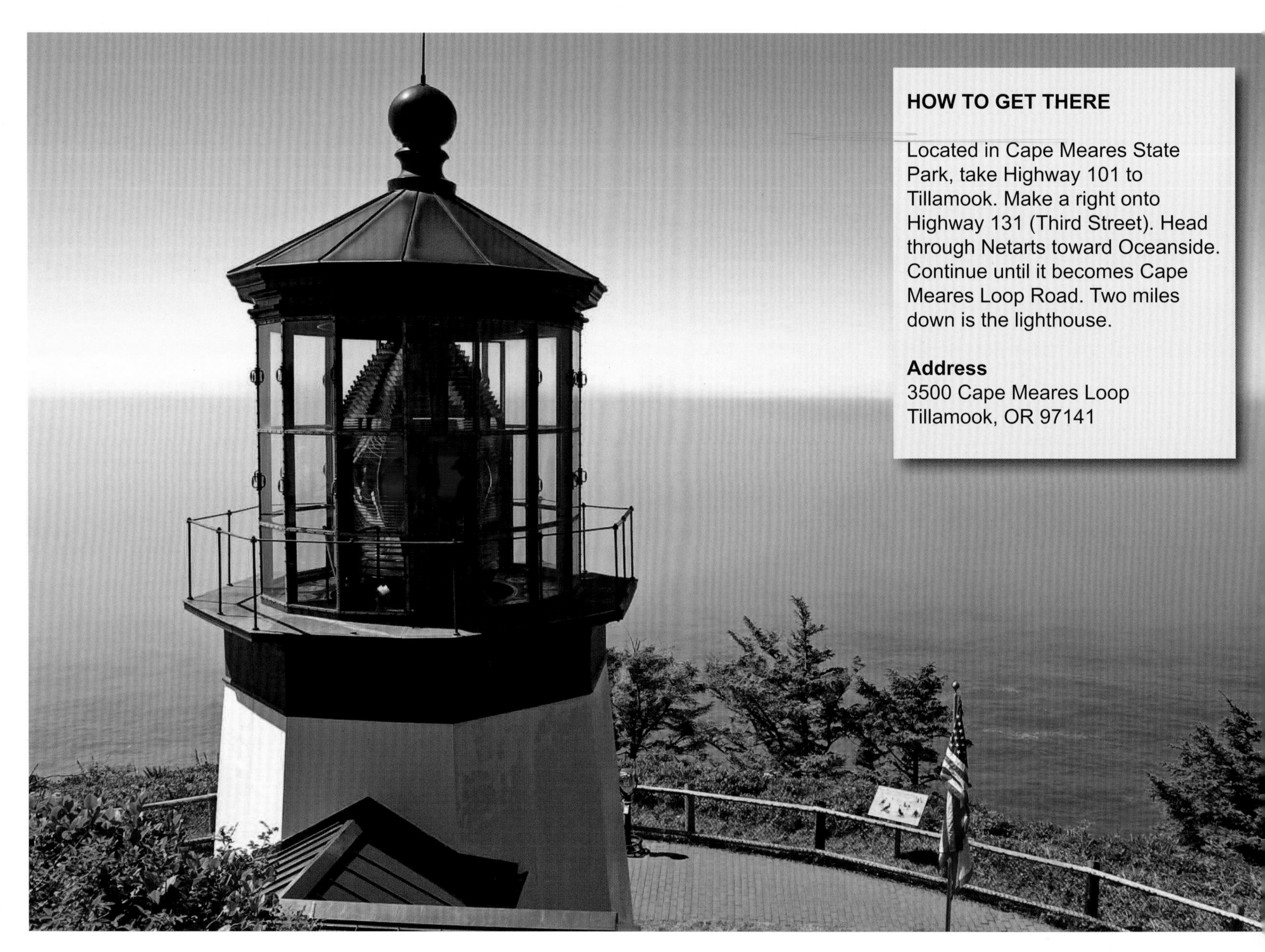

HOW TO GET THERE

Located in Cape Meares State Park, take Highway 101 to Tillamook. Make a right onto Highway 131 (Third Street). Head through Netarts toward Oceanside. Continue until it becomes Cape Meares Loop Road. Two miles down is the lighthouse.

Address
3500 Cape Meares Loop
Tillamook, OR 97141

COQUILLE RIVER LIGHT

Built: 1895
Style: Brick
Height: 40 feet (12.19m)

This shorter beacon is one of eleven lighthouses left in Oregon. It operated until 1939, shutting down earlier than most because of a depressed economy that led to less shipping demands. Because of this, the light was extinguished and unused for twenty-four years, a time period longer than the light was in active service.

Before construction began, engineers needed to level the rocky tip so that the lighthouse could be constructed on a flat base. Local rock was used for the base of the tower, while the tower itself was built with brick. A layer of heavy stucco was added for additional protection. During its heyday, a Fresnel lens illuminated a solid, white light over the waters. Some years later, a fog trumpet steam signal was added to the site to blast every thirty seconds. Oil engines and compressed air created the steamy sound, which lasted five seconds with each blast. A massive, 5,000-gallon water tank was also added to the property to increase the water needed to operate the signal. It was placed on top of an eight-foot trestle. Two short years later, rough waters toppled the tank and washed it away. It was eventually replaced and better secured with steel beams.

It wasn't until the 1970s when Oregon State Parks, in conjunction with the Army Corps of Engineers, used funds allocated for restoration to bring the lighthouse back to life on the rocky jetty. A light is still on in the tower today, but it is not used for navigation.

LEFT & RIGHT: The Coquille River Light has undergone a restoration project to bring it back to its former glory.

HOW TO GET THERE

Located in Bullards Beach State Park, the lighthouse grounds are open to visitors May through September. While the lighthouse is not accessible to view, the fog room is. To get there, Take US 101 north to the park on Coquille River. Turn onto Park Road. At the fork in the road, head right toward the water.

Address
56487 Bullards Beach Rd.
Bandon, OR 97411

ELDRED ROCK LIGHT

Built: 1906
Style: Octagonal, House-Style
Height: 56 feet (17.06m)

When the steamer Clara Nevada crashed and burned along the rocks of the Lynn Canal in 1898, more than 100 passengers drowned near Eldred Rock. Also washed away was $1,000,000 in gold. It was the peak of the Alaskan gold rush and it was a devastating loss. The tragedy was enough to prove that the Northwestern end of the Alaska Panhandle needed a guiding light. The site of the crash is a popular dive site but, to date, not a trace of gold has ever been found.

The structure was built as a house with a tower protruding out of the center of it. The sloping red roof topped the bottom of the dwelling, which was made of concrete. Keepers and their families settled in the eight-room home. The upper portion and the lighthouse was made of wood, including the lantern room that housed a Fresnel lens. Next to the keeper's dwelling was a fog signal, fed by water and manned by the keeper himself. Just 300 feet north of the octagonal structure was a boathouse.

The site itself was just about two and a half acres, and while the house and tower was only 56 feet, the focal plane of the beacon was more than ninety feet above water. It was, and still is, a sturdy structure. During a particularly windy storm in 1908, the lighthouse keeper tucked he and his family safely inside while the gale winds pounded outside. When he emerged the next day, he was stunned to see the remains of the Clara Nevada stranded on the island. The winds had pulled it up from the ocean floor. It slowly sunk again later that night.

The beacon is not a working lighthouse at this time. It is maintained by the Eldred Rock Lighthouse Preservation Association which is currently raising funds to undergo preservation.

RIGHT: Eldred Rock Lighthouse is the oldest original lighthouse in Alaska.

HOW TO GET THERE

The lighthouse is not open to the public, but it can be seen by a boat tour secured by the Sheldon Museum & Cultural Center. To get to the center, head south on Alaska Marine Highway-Skagway. Make a left on Lutak Road. Go about four miles, and make a left onto Beach Road/AK-7. Turn right onto Main Street.

Address
Sheldon Museum & Cultural Center
11 Main St.
Haines, AK 99827

HOW TO GET THERE

The lighthouse is open to the public and can be seen from Ocean Avenue in Westport. To get there, take US-101 South to WA-105. Make a right onto South Forrest Street WA-105 spur. After about two miles, make a right on West Ocean Avenue.

Address
Grays Harbor Lighthouse
1020 West Ocean Ave.
Westport, WA 98595

GRAYS HARBOR LIGHT

Built: 1898
Style: Octagonal, Brick
Range: 21 miles (33.79km)
Height: 107 feet (32.61m)

Nestled inside a forest of deep green conifers, this mammoth lighthouse on Point Chehalis serves as a major coastal lighthouse on the Pacific coast. The structure sufficiently marks the entrance of the bay which is shaped like an arrowhead. At just over one hundred feet, the light is the tallest in all of Washington. The harbor itself was discovered by Captain Robert Gray (thus the name), a Boston fur trader who scoped out the land in 1792. However, some ninety years would pass before a lighthouse would be erected there.

It was 1884 when Congress approved funding for the beacon. However, discussions kept the light from being constructed. When it was realized that a much larger light needed to be built, more funds were allocated in 1886. Despite the additional cash, it still wasn't enough. Each year, the Lighthouse Board applied for more cash until a contract was drafted for a light to be built, not to exceed $75,000. Construction began in 1897. A Fresnel lens was installed in 1898.

Today, the lighthouse is open to the public. However, it was closed for a few years during the 1990s due to health concerns when it was considered that a mercury-filled drum could be dangerous. The Westport-South Beach Historical Society maintains the property and is currently working to further restore all of the buildings on site.

LEFT: Gray's Harbor Light marks the best of Washington's few outer-coast harbors.

HECETA HEAD LIGHT

Built: 1894
Style: Masonry
Range: 21 miles (33.79km)
Height: 56 feet (17.06m)

Before the turn of the century, there wasn't a single light along the 90-mile stretch between Cape Foulweather and Cape Argo. When it was determined that the cliffs of Heceta Head needed to be illuminated, a hefty sum of $180,000 was allocated to build it. Construction took two years, thanks to the extreme remoteness of the location. Materials had to be shipped from the Suislaw River and then carried the rest of the way on a wagon pulled by mules. Once the lighthouse was done, it was brilliant.

The light at the top was a Fresnel lens built with 640 prisms. It was hand-cranked with a cable and gears. The first keeper had a long walk to arrive at his post. Andrew P.C. Hald had to make his way eighteen miles to Astoria. From there he took a train to Newport where he had to walk another twenty-four miles to the lighthouse. The trip was exhausting and took days. His wife still hadn't arrived with the furniture, as she took a different route on the water via ship. Life for the keeper was not easy. Because of the extreme isolation, there was no medical care. When his wife suffered a long-term illness, there were no doctors to care for her. His young baby died, too, because there was no care for miles.

Because of how remote the lighthouse and dwelling were, a schoolhouse was built on site so the children of the keepers could be properly educated. Things are much different now and access to the jagged point is much easier. Today, the Heceta Head Light is one of the few in North America that has been turned into a bed and breakfast. It is a popular destination for weddings and other events.

HOW TO GET THERE

From Interstate 5, head from the California border. Take the 195B Santa Clara/Florence exit. Turn onto Beltline Road. When the road ends, make a right onto Highway 126 toward Florence. After sixty miles, make a right onto Highway 101. Signs for the destination are on the highway.

Address
92072 US-101 South
Yachats, OR 97498

RIGHT: Constructed in 1894, the Heceta Head Light was named after the Spanish explorer Don Bruno de Heceta. Its beacon, visible for more than 20 miles out at sea, is the most powerful on the Oregon coast.

KILAUEA POINT LIGHT

Built: 1913
Style: Conical, Concrete
Height: 52 feet (15.84m)

HOW TO GET THERE

The lighthouse is open to the public and is inside of the Kilauea Point National Wildlife Refuge. To get there from Lihue, head north on Kuhio Highway for 23 miles toward Kilauea. Make a right onto Kolo Road, and then make a left on Kilauea Road. After two miles, see the refuge entrance and parking area.

Address
3500 Kilauea Rd.
Kilauea, HI 96754

Some lighthouses face major challenges during construction and Kilauea Point is one of them. When materials arrived on a vessel, workers discovered the structure couldn't be built without digging through the earth first. Eleven feet later, they hit rock. In order to safely anchor a lighthouse on the point and into the earth, the original plans of the lighthouse had to change. As a result, the structure has a basement. This makes the Kilauea light unique, as basements are a very rare feature in these mini-castles.

Construction began with a metal frame and outer concrete housing in 1912. The frame was built in Ohio. When the lighthouse was done, it served many ships, guiding them safely through the waters from its rocky cliff. It also aided one of the first flights from Hawaii's mainland. In 1927, an airplane struggled to find its way in the dark sky. It wasn't until the men inside the plane saw the light of the tower below that they were able to determine where they were. They stayed close to the beacon for several hours until daylight and then resumed their flight back home.

After the attack on Pearl Harbor, the light was dark for the remainder of the war. It became automated in 1974. For years, the lighthouse sat in disrepair and then in April of 2007, $1 million dollars was raised to restore the lighthouse and open it to the public.

LEFT & INSET: Kilauea Point Light stands in a nature reserve which is one of the few places where seabirds such as the red-footed booby, laysan albatross, and wedge-tailed shearwater can be found. Seals, whales, and turtles can also be seen from the reserve.

LIME KILN LIGHT

Built: 1914
Style: Concrete, House-Style
Height: 38 feet (11.58m)

One of five lights that exist on the San Juan Islands in the Pacific Northwest, the Lime Kiln Light shines atop a chain of 172 islands that populate the Haro straits between Washington State and Canada. The islands offer a web of narrow passages and dangerous rocks, making the light and its four brothers necessary. The other lights on the Islands are: Turn Point Light (1893), Patos Island Light (1908), Barrows Island Light (1906), and Cattle Point Light (1935).

Lime Kiln is on the western side of San Juan and was one of the last major lights established in Washington State. Still a navigational aid to mariners, the light also serves as a whale research center. The area is home to several orcas, or killer whales. Because the lighthouse is so close to the shoreline, experts can set up microphones in the water and squat on site to hear the whales.

The thirty-eight-foot octagonal tower sits atop a connected fog signal building that still emits a white light every ten seconds. There are two dwellings on site, both of which are used to house park staff. The light didn't become automated until well after World War II, making it the last lighthouse in Washington to be lit without the aid of a keeper.

BELOW & RIGHT: When the weather is good, the Olympic Mountains and Vancouver Island can be seen from Lime Kiln Light.

HOW TO GET THERE

Because the lighthouse is used for whale research, the light is closed to the public. It can be viewed, however, from Lime Kiln Point State Park. Here, many come to see the whales and view the lighthouse. To get there, take the Lopez Island Ferry. From the ferry, head down Front Street. At the fork bear left. Make a quick left onto Spring Street, which will eventually become San Juan Valley Road. Make a left onto Douglas Road and then a slight right onto Bailer Hill Road. Bailer Hill Road will become Westside Road, which will then become Lime Kiln Point State Park. Stay right to enter the park.

Address
Lime Kiln Point State Park
1567 Westside Rd.
Friday Harbor
San Juan Island, WA 98250

HOW TO GET THERE

The lighthouse and grounds are open to the public April through September. To get there, take I-94 west and get off at exit 27 toward St. Cloud. You will pass through North Dakota and into Montana. Eventually, I-94 will become I-90 as you enter Washington State. Merge onto I-405 north, then take exit 10 toward Bellevue/Everett. Continue straight onto WA-525 north. After eight miles make a left onto Front Street.

Address
608 Front St.
Mukilteo, WA 98275

MUKILTEO LIGHT

Built: 1906
Style: Victorian, Wood
Height: 30 feet (9.14m)

This white and red colored lighthouse with an attached fog signal room was named for a Snohomish Indian word meaning "good camping place." Before it was a light station, it was where Governor Isaac Stevens and several Puget Sound tribes met to create what is known as the Treaty of Point Elliott. Eleven years after the treaty was signed the structure was built.

The original site also included two homes for lighthouse keepers and a windmill that supplied water for the entire town of Mukilteo. The windmill needed a 1,000-gallon tank to feed it, and it was housed in a separate building that was also a workshop and coal room. The multi-purpose light station was originally built with two Fresnel lenses, one of which had bullseye panels.

Most lighthouses today still function with their original Fresnel lens. The Mukilteo light is one of them. When the US Coast Guard wanted to upgrade the light with an aero-marine beacon, area residents protested and were heard. This classic beacon today flashes with its antique light every five seconds. The lighthouse is a popular destination for weddings. Legend has it that it has never rained during any wedding ceremony. The lighthouse was officially automated in 1927. Because the beacon is so popular, lighthouse lovers can now get a Washington license plate with the iconic lighthouse on it when they renew their registration.

LEFT & BELOW: In 2001, the US Coast Guard turned over ownership of Mukilteo Light to the City of Mukilteo. It is the centerpiece of Mukilteo Lighthouse Park and open to the public.

NEW DUNGENESS LIGHT

Built: 1857
Style: Conical
Height: 63 feet (19.20m)

The New Dungeness Light stands on the edge of the eight-mile-long Dungeness Spit, boasting a tale that isn't nearly as tall as the tower once was. When it was originally built, the lighthouse was actually thirty-seven feet taller than it is today. But due to poor construction, the danger of collapse was imminent. Engineers solved the problem by cutting the top of the tower off.

The light served many who navigated the waters at Dungeness Spit, including the Indian warriors who would meet there to resolve their conflicts. After the lighthouse was erected in 1857, the Indians continued to meet on the spit, using the light as their guide. Rarely was a conflict settled that wasn't bloody. Thankfully, they never went after the lighthouse keepers during their "meetings."

Dungeness Spit takes its name from Dungeness Point in England, noted for being a treacherous area for ships. The number of vessels doomed on the state side is also endless. While the bright Fresnel lens alerted ships of potential danger, it couldn't slow them down as they plowed into the rocks and shoals ahead of them. Between the angry natives and the doomed ships, it seemed the area between Port Townsend and Port Angeles was a danger for man all the way around. Today, that danger is gone, but the stories, tales, and history makes this light so interesting.

BELOW & RIGHT: The lighthouse, the keeper's quarters, and three other properties at the site were added to the National Register of Historic Places in 1993.

HOW TO GET THERE

The lighthouse is open to the public and is free, although donations are appreciated. To get there, take US 101 to Kitchen-Dick Road. Continue on Kitchen-Dick Road for about three miles until you see the Dungeness National Wildlife Refuge. Drive into the refuge on Voice of America Road West and until you reach the parking lot. There is a five-mile hike following to reach the lighthouse. It can also be reached by boat.

Address
Dungeness National Wildlife Refuge
554 Voice of America Rd. West
Sequim, WA 98382

OLD POINT LOMA LIGHT

Built: 1855
Style: Cape Cod-style, Sandstone
Height: 40 feet (12.19m)

Not to be confused with Point Loma Light also at the same location, Old Point Loma Light was erected as one of the first lighthouse stations on the West Coast after the US acquired California from Spain. Built with the tower protruding from the keeper's dwelling, the structure cost the government a whopping $30,000 to build. Little did the Lighthouse Board know that that price would give them more than they asked for.

To begin with, the lighthouse was built shoddily. So when a fourth-order Fresnel lens was shipped to the point for installation, it didn't fit. A different Fresnel lens had to be shipped over, causing a delay in the lighting of the tower. When it did arrive, the light was bright enough to be seen for up to forty miles at 460 feet above sea level. And while that sounds like it would serve the ships on the water, it didn't. It turned out that the light shone above low-lying clouds and fog banks, making it difficult for sailors to see it clearly. It wasn't until 1891 that the problem was finally solved when a second skeletal tower (Point Loma Light) was built on the same site. After thirty-six years in service, the Old Point Loma Light was distinguished permanently.

Despite its darkness, the lighthouse was still used over the years. During World War II, soldiers painted the lighthouse camouflage green and used it as a signal tower to help direct ships into the harbor. Today, the tower has been refurbished back to its original state and is open to the public within the borders of the Cabrillo National Monument.

THESE PAGES: Today, Old Point Loma Lighthouse is the centerpiece of Cabrillo National Monument, commanding spectacular views over San Diego Bay.

HOW TO GET THERE

To get to Cabrillo National Monument, take CA-163 South to Exit 12. After eight miles, take Exit 3B toward until Nimitz Boulevard Continue for several miles until Chatsworth Boulevard. Make a left onto Catalina Boulevard. Catalina Boulevard eventually becomes Cabrillo Memorial Drive.

Address
Cabrillo National Monument
1800 Cabrillo Memorial Dr.
San Diego, CA 92106

PIGEON POINT LIGHT

Built: 1871
Style: Conical, Brick
Height: 115 feet (35.05m)

Perched high on a bluff above the Pacific Ocean sits Pigeon Point Light, now part of a hostel that accommodates overnight visitors. But before it became a point of interest, Pigeon Point was a much needed light station on the jagged bluff. The tower was named after the clipper ship Carrier Pigeon, which crashed into the rocks and sunk in 1853. It wasn't the first shipwreck and it wouldn't be the last. After at least a dozen ships met their fate here, Congress agreed to allocate funds to build a tower. To date, it is the tallest tower on the West Coast next to Point Arena Tower.

Located about fifty miles south of San Francisco, the light was equipped with a radio antenna so that Morse code could be used, a feature that was unique to the station. Eventually, the code was synced with the fog signal so that Captains could hear the delay between the two sounds. This enabled them to better navigate safely around the light. The light was automated in 1974, and the fog signal disabled in 1976.

The area attracts curious tourists, thanks to the number of seals and whales that make regular appearances. The lighthouse itself is closed for repairs. In the winter of 2001, part of the exterior of the lighthouse fell to the ground. Until restoration is completed, the structure can only be viewed from the outside. The houses on the site where visitors stay are not original lightkeeper houses but were built by the US Coast Guard in 1960. The four ranch-style homes can accommodate up to 14 people per house.

HOW TO GET THERE

History walks are available on weekends. To get to the tower, take I-80 W toward San Francisco. Merge onto US-101 S/James Lick Freeway South via exit 1A toward San Jose, then merge onto I-280 S via exit 431 toward Daly City. Keep right and prepare to take the CA-1 via exit 47B toward Pacifica. Turn right onto Pigeon Point Road.

Address
210 Pigeon Point Rd./Highway 1
Pescadero, CA 94060

ABOVE & RIGHT: Because no elevated site was available in the area, Pigeon Point's tower was made uncharacteristically tall for a light on the West Coast.

POINT BONITA LIGHT

Built: 1877
Style: Conical, Iron
Height: 33 feet (10.05m)

Pointing the way to Golden Gate, the original beacon built on this point in 1855 was so important to mariners, that Congress made sure it housed a second-order Fresnel lens; one of the brightest and most expensive. But much like the short-lived Old Point Loma Light, low-lying clouds and heavy fog made this particular light impossible to see. To offset the issue, a cannon was brought on site to be fired during foggy days and nights. It was eventually replaced by a 1,500-pound bell.

In 1872 officials recognized that a new lighthouse in the San Francisco Bay was in order and decided to build the current structure closer to the water where the light would prove more effective. What the Lighthouse Board didn't account for was how difficult construction would be.

Contractors began to work out the logistics of building the light on the narrow ledge that jutted out some 120 feet above the waves. They determined that the only way to successfully get materials to the ledge was to blast a tunnel through the rock, and then build a platform and incline that could reach the tunnel. It took five years to complete the tower and the buildings that enclosed two steam-driven fog sirens. But when it was done it was a blessing to mariners.

Today, a suspension bridge connects the lighthouse to the fog-signal building. Point Bonita is the only lighthouse in America that has such a feature. The bridge was built after a landslide destroyed the original wooden bridge sometime in the 1940s. Now part of the Golden Gate National Recreation Area, the lighthouse is visited by thousands of tourists each year. The light is still active and maintained by the US Coast Guard.

THESE PAGES: Point Bonita sits precariously on a rocky outcrop. Building was started 1872 and lasted for five years. It replaced an earlier light that proved ineffective in fog.

HOW TO GET THERE

The lighthouse itself is not open to the public, except on Sundays, but it can be viewed from a short distance. Visitors can take Highway 101, north of San Francisco over the Golden Gate Bridge. Exit at Alexander Avenue onto Conzelman Road. Continue on this winding road until you reach the lighthouse. Prepare for a mile walk to get there.

Address
Golden Gate National Recreation Area
Sausalito, CA 94965

POINT CABRILLO LIGHT

Built: 1909
Style: House-style, Wooden
Height: 47 feet (14.32m)

Many lighthouses along dark coastlines were quite secluded, leaving lighthouse keepers and their families to fend for themselves when it came to medical emergencies and educating their children. But the Point Cabrillo Light was different. With close access to churches, schools, and stores, life for the keeper wasn't as trying. Even still, they worked hard to maintain equipment and keep the light glowing.

The house-style dwelling, combined with the protruding lighthouse on top of it, looks similar to an old-style church. Attached to the structure is the fog-signal building, once run with an eighteen-horsepower engine that set off two loud sirens when the fog with thick. The Fresnel lens that was installed in the lantern room revolved every two minutes and sent a white flash of light over the waters every ten seconds.

The last lighthouse keeper to maintain the light left in 1963. At that time the US Coast Guard took over until the light was automated in the 1970s. The antiquated Fresnel lens was turned off and a more modern light took its place. But this new light was mounted on the roof of the lantern room. The original lens sat inside the lantern room covered all the while, until the Coast Guard announced its intention to relocate it to a museum in Virginia. But the public wouldn't have it, and it 1991 the California State Coastal Conservancy bought the land and the light, eventually collaborating with the North Coast Interpretive Association to preserve the historic site. Despite the switch in property owners, the light is still an active aid of navigation for the US Coast Guard today.

BELOW & RIGHT: Cabrillo Point Light is one of three that are situated on the Point Loma Peninsula. The other two are Old Point Loma Lighthouse and New Point Loma Lighthouse.

HOW TO GET THERE

From Lakeville Highway/CA-116, continue until it turns into Lakeville Street. Make a left onto East Washington Street. Eventually, East Washington Street becomes Bodega Ave and then Bodega Avenue becomes Valley Ford Road. After ten miles or so, Valley Ford Road becomes CA-1/S Highway. Continue onto South Highway 1/CA-1 until School Street. From there, make a slight left onto Lighthouse Road.

Address
45300 Lighthouse Rd.
Mendocino, CA 95460

HOW TO GET THERE

The lighthouse is open to the public for tours. To reach the house, take CA-91 W/Artesia Freeway West via Exit 7A. After the exit, take the I-110 S exit, Exit 6, toward San Pedro. Merge onto I-110 S/Harbor Freeway S. Prepare to take the exit on the left. Make a left onto North Gaffey Street and then a right onto West Paseo del Mar. West Paseo del Mar is just west of Pacific Avenue.

Address
807 West Paseo Del Mar
San Pedro, CA 90731

POINT FERMIN LIGHT

Built: 1874
Style: Victorian House-style, Wood
Height: 30 feet (9.14m)

When the San Pedro Bay grew dark at night, vessels and ships moved cautiously over the waves to avoid danger. It took the drive of a local businessman to call on government officials to place a beacon on the point. It was 1854 when the Lighthouse Board agreed. However, due to lots of government red tape and land disputes, the funding didn't show up for another twenty years. Once things were rectified, construction on the architectural marvel began in 1874.

The structure was one of six lighthouses designed the same way. Today, only three of this style remain. This particular structure was built with durable redwood and is considered a Victorian-era Italianate, complete with gabled roofs and gingerbread trim. But most interesting about this lighthouse is the first keepers. They were women, which was highly unusual in the late 19th century. Mary and Ella Smith were familiar with the lifestyle of the lighthouse keeper because some of their family members manned different lights along the coast. So when they took the job, no doubt with help of their brother who was a customs officer at the time, they managed it quite successfully for eight years.

After the sisters left their post it was filled by retired sea captain, George Shaw. Because the house was such a sight, many local residents found their way to West Paseo Del Mar to marvel at it. The Lighthouse Board encouraged Captain Shaw to provide eager residents with tours of the house. The tradition continued with the Shaw family of lightkeepers that took over after the captain retired. They raised their children, served the community, and manned the lighthouse until the beacon became automated in 1927. It remained automated until the attack on Pearl Harbor in 1941. Like many lighthouses during the war, the light was darkened to prevent enemy ships or planes from finding their way. The lighthouse was restored in 2002 with the help of Los Angeles, the Port of Los Angeles, and the State of California.

LEFT & BELOW: The architecture of Point Fermin Light is ornate and very attractive. The lighthouse has now been fully restored and is a tourist attraction within Point Fermin City Park.

POINT PINOS LIGHT

Built: 1855
Style: House-Style, Granite
Height: 43 feet (13.10m)

Surrounded by a beautiful golf course, the West's oldest lighthouse once sat quietly on the jagged rocks of the Monterey Peninsula. It was built by Francis Gibbons, a well-known lighthouse contractor, who originally constructed the building with granite. But after the 1906 earthquake that rocked San Francisco, the dwelling and tower needed to be reinforced with concrete.

Like most lighthouses of the day, the lantern room was dressed with a Fresnel lens. Shipped to the site and installed in 1855, the light rotated on a shutter which forced the light to blink on for ten seconds and off for twenty. The same lens still lights up the waterways in the Monterey Peninsula, only now the light flashes electronically every four seconds. When lighthouse keepers weren't maintaining the lantern room or cleaning the prisms on the lens, they were hiking three miles into town to gather goods for the remote dwelling. It was a dangerous hike, considering bears and cougars were aplenty. Because of this, some supplies were delivered by ship.

The Point Pinos light has some interesting history. The first lighthouse keeper was part of a gang, and after he died of a gunshot wound, his wife was assigned to take over the duties. Thanks to the people of Monterey, Mrs. Charlotte Layton was able to man the post at the tower so that she could continue to take care of her four children. She was the very first lighthouse keeper on the West Coast.

HOW TO GET THERE

The grounds of the lighthouse are open to the public for a small donation. Interested visitors should take Highway 1 and get off at exit 399A/Pebble Beach/Pacific Grove/68 West. From there, follow Highway 68. Eventually, Highway 68 will become Forest Avenue. Continue on Forest Avenue until downtown Pacific Grove. Make a left onto Lighthouse Avenue. Turn right onto Asilomar Avenue.

Address
80 Asilomar Ave
Pacific Grove, CA 93950

RIGHT: Built in the 1850s, Point Pinos is the oldest lighthouse still operating in America.

POINT ROBINSON LIGHT

Built: 1915
Style: Cylindrical, Concrete
Range: 12 miles (19.31km)
Height: 38 feet (11.58m)

Mariners who traveled along Puget Sound between Seattle and Tacoma relied on the Point Robinson Light located on the eastern end of Maury Island to guide them safely through the narrow waterways. Some days saw heavier traffic than others. It was when the ships were aplenty and the fog thick that sailors truly sensed trouble.

Before the first lighthouse was erected in 1887, a fog signal was placed on site in 1885 to prevent ships from running aground. During one particular foggy night, the keeper on site had to sound the whistle for 528 hours. Despite the loud horn, ships continued to unintentionally drive their massive vessels up onto the sandy spit that extended out into Puget Sound. Even the skeletal structure with a glowing light on top couldn't save the ships from grounding. It was then that the Lighthouse Board agreed to fund construction for a new lighthouse.

In 1915, the current lighthouse was established. Three keeper's dwellings were part of the blueprint, as well as the lighthouse and existing fog signal building constructed as one. Whales were a common sight here and lightkeepers often logged their appearances. Most notably was when a whale became stranded on the shoal near the point. The lighthouse keeper and his assistant didn't want to see the massive animal struggle, and so they pulled large planks to where it lay and pushed them up against the whale. Soon enough, it started to float and swam its way back out to sea.

HOW TO GET THERE

Tours of the lighthouse start in mid-May and end in mid-September. To reach the historical and marine conservancy where it stands, take the Fauntleroy-Vashon Ferry. Upon arrival, head south on Vashon Highway SW. Turn left onto Dugway Road South. Then turn left onto SW Quartermaster Drive. From here, turn right onto Dockton Road SW. Continue onto SW Point Robinson Road. Turn right to stay on SW Point Robinson Road.

Address
3705 SW Point Robinson Rd.
Vashon Island, WA 98070

RIGHT: The Point Robinson Light is located on the easternmost point of Maury Island, in the southeastern Puget Sound. Seattle can be seen just across the water to the north.

POINT VICENTE LIGHT

Built: 1926
Style: Cylindrical
Range: 20 miles (32.18km)
Height: 67 feet (20.42m)

Looming among the palms on a cliff high above the waves of the Pacific Ocean sits the brilliant Point Vicente Light. The visual of this structure is so aesthetic that the light has been used as a backdrop for countless Hollywood films and television shows. The cross-hatched windows surrounding the lantern room only adds to the lighthouses glory, continuing to emit its glow with the original Fresnel lens. Unlike most lighthouses, this structure didn't have a nearby dwelling for its keepers. Those manning the tower and their families lived in nearby cottages.

Hundreds of lighthouses across North America have ghost stories to share and the Point Vicente Light is one of them. Residents share the story of the ladylike figure who shows herself on the foggiest of nights. She was the lover of a sailor who died in a shipwreck near the point. Some

non-believers say her image is merely an illusion created by the reflection off of the cross-hatched windows. When the residents of the area began to complain about the light being a hazard to drivers, the inside of the windows were painted white to dim it. Shortly thereafter, the haunting figure of the woman would show up on the tower's walkway, pacing back and forth.

HOW TO GET THERE

The lighthouse is not open to the public at this time but can be seen from the nearby Palos Verdes Interpretive Center. To get there, take the Pacific Coast Highway/CA-1 and get off at Exit 4. Turn right onto West Pacific Coast Highway/CA-1. Make a left onto Crenshaw Boulevard. Turn right onto Crest Road and then left onto Hawthorne Boulevard/CA-107. Continue to follow Hawthorne Boulevard. Turn left onto Palos Verdes Drive West to reach the lighthouse.

Address
31550 Palos Verdes Dr. West
Rancho Palos Verdes, CA 90274

LEFT & ABOVE: The Point Vicente Light's romantic looks have made it a favorite setting for movies and commercials. More importantly, however, is the fact that it has been saving lives for over 80 years.

YAQUINA HEAD LIGHT

Built: 1873
Style: Conical, Brick
Height: 93 feet (28.34m)

Some lighthouses attract photographers from all over the world because of their immeasurable beauty and fascinating history. The Yaquina Head light is one such light. The tall, white structure stands on a cliff of dark rock which is literally a massive magnet. Compasses and radios go haywire when they approach the beacon because at the core the rock is magnetized iron. Despite the light that illuminates at the top of the cliff, the magnetism alone has caused dozens of ships to ground, claiming the lives of hundreds.

Why would the Lighthouse Board build a tower in such a dangerous location? Original plans called for the construction of the tower at Cape Foulweather. But the magnetic rock likely messed up navigation and crews mistakenly landed at Yaquina Head instead. They set about their work and erected the tower without incident. When the board discovered

HOW TO GET THERE

Guided tours of the lighthouse are available. To view the structure, take I-5 S/Pacific Highway 1 South toward Salem. Merge onto OR-99W from Exit 294 toward Tigard/Newberg. Make a left onto OR-18/OR-233/SE Dayton Bypass. Continue to follow OR-18 and then make a slight right onto North Highway 101/US-101 S. Continue to follow US-101 South. After 27 miles, turn right onto NW Lighthouse Drive.

Address
750 NW Lighthouse Dr.
Newport, OR 97365

he mistake, they decided to keep the tower in place and deactivate the nearby Yaquina Bay Lighthouse. The original lighthouse still stands oday, greeting boaters, vessels, and curious lighthouse aficionados.

BELOW & RIGHT: The Yaquina Bay Light is one of the West Coast's oldest lighthouses. The station was automated in 1966, and is now maintained by Oregon State Parks.

LIGHTHOUSES OF CANADA

The lighthouses of Canada are as diverse as they are beautiful, enhancing the sunsets along the world's longest coastline. Left in existence are roughly 750 of the historic structures, some still hugging the shores of Lake Ontario and the coasts of Newfoundland. Many stand at the mouth of the Saint Lawrence River and the Bay of Fundy, too. Today, Canada is working diligently to ensure that as many structures as possible are restored in an effort to preserve the heritage and history for the benefit of Canadians everywhere.

BACCARO POINT LIGHT

Built: 1934
Style: Square Pyramidal, Wood
Height: 44 feet (13.41m)

Nestled on a solid bed of rock along the inlet of Barrington Bay sits Baccaro Point Light. The name of the light itself comes from the Basque word *Baccolaos* and means codfish. The first lighthouse here was built in 1852 and required hard labor from the crew who not only had to haul heavy materials along the beach to get to the site but spent long days building it as well.

The first lighthouse keeper, James S. Smith, was involved in the laborious construction. Sitting on the southernmost point of the Nova Scotia mainland, the first tower he helped erect was painted with black rings so that it could be distinguished from other nearby towers. When the work on the tower was complete, Smith decided the single tower wasn't enough. On his own, the ambitious keeper built three more buildings on site; a storehouse, a workshop, and a barn. Smith used the workshop to cobble shoes to help supplement his income.

For many years, the original tower served mariners, but after a fire compromised the tower in 1934, the present 44-foot one was built. The last keeper retired in 1984 and in the same year the old keeper's dwelling was pulled down and the station automated. One of the buildings to survive was needed on Seal Point and so was moved. Today, efforts are being made to preserve the lighthouse.

HOW TO GET THERE

The lighthouse is closed to the public but can still be visited. To reach the historic landmark, take Route 103 in Clyde River. Then take Route 309 south. Look for signs that point you toward the Baccaro Lighthouse. Continue about 16 miles (25.8km) to Lighthouse Road. Continue on the gravel road to the parking lot.

Address
Lighthouse Rd.
Barrington, NS B0W 2A0

RIGHT: Baccaro Point Light is perched at the edge of the ocean. It is an important seabird watching site.

BADDECK HARBOUR/KIDSTON ISLAND LIGHT

Built: 1875
Style: Square Pyramidal, Wood
Height: 48 feet (14.5m)

Overlooking the saltwater lake of Bras d'Or, this low structure light marks the entrance of Baddeck, a cozy resort town located in Cape Breton Highlands. History books show that Alexander Graham Bell once had a summer home there. A museum in the town offers memorabilia and stories on his life. His mansion is still there, and it is a focal point for visitors of the resort.

The lighthouse is interchangeably called the Kidston Island Light or the Baddeck Harbour Light. Locals refer to it as the Baddeck Harbour Light. Before the current structure was built, a different lighthouse was erected in 1875. It served mariners until 1912, when the current structure was built. The new tower was equipped with a Fresnel lens. For a while, the two towers stood side by side. Today, only the red and white tower still exists, visible by boat or from downtown Baddeck.

HOW TO GET THERE

The lighthouse is closed to the public but can be viewed from downtown Baddeck or via a boat tour. Amoeba Sailing Tours at the end of the Baddeck Community Wharf is an excellent way to view it. To get there, take MA-3 S/Pilgrims Highway via Exit 7 toward Cape Cod. Merge onto MA-139. After about five miles, make a left onto Winslow Street. A short distance down, make a left onto Jones Road. See the Baddeck Community Wharf. Parking is available.

Address
Baddeck
NS B0E 1B0

LEFT & BELOW: The lighthouse can only be accessed by boat; a ferry operates during the summer months.

BRIER ISLAND LIGHT

Built: 1944
Style: Octagonal, Concrete
Height: 60 feet (18.28m)

For the lights of Brier Island, third time's a charm. Brier Island isn't a big island. Just four miles long and two miles wide, the tiny jagged island rock with its bold beacon has helped navigate big ships since the first light was raised on a clunky wooden tower in 1807. The light served its purpose to the best of its ability but had to be rebuilt in 1832. This second light was also wooden but built a bit sturdier with a metal lantern. Much

BELOW LEFT & BELOW: Brier Island is infamous for its foggy weather and consequently is also the site of many shipwrecks.

HOW TO GET THERE

The lighthouse is not open to the public but can be viewed from the grounds. To visit, take NS-217/Highway 217 to the Westport Ferry. Once off the ferry, head southwest on Water Street. Make a right onto Wellington Street West. Continue to Lighthouse Road.

Address
720 Lighthouse Rd.
Digby, NS B0V 1A0

ike today's tower, it was painted with red rings. Three, to be precise, to elp daytime mariners see it clearly. A fog signal building was also constructed to help guide ships on unclear nights.

Sometime in 1905, the dwelling for the lighthouse keepers was also built. Salaries were low for the hard-working men, but at $400 a year, keepers here were seeing a bit more than those in the states. Two men were on site at this time, one to man the tower and the other to manage he fog whistle.

In 1944 tragedy struck the second tower when it caught fire and burned to the ground. This is when the candy cane colored mini-castle was built at the southern end of Digby Neck overlooking the entrance of St. Marys. This is the Bay of Fundy, where high tides and big ships are a common sight. Until 1972, lighthouse keepers managed the site. The lighthouse became fully automated in 1987. The tower is painted with the daymark of red stripes so that it can still be seen in the whitest of snows.

BROCKTON POINT LIGHT

Built: 1914
Style: Quadrangular, Concrete
Height: 34 feet (10.36m)

The Brockton Point Light is a magnet for tourists from all over the world. Its history is rich and begins with the first ever light erected in Stanley Park in 1890. As the railroad was being constructed and shipping traffic on the water began to grow, it was clear that the Prospect Point Lighthouse near the First Narrows on the Pacific Ocean wasn't enough. Vessels coming into Vancouver needed more guidance and it seemed that further lighting up the dark waterways of the British Columbia coast would be the answer. With a simple mast and lanterns, an unsturdy light was erected at Brockton Point. The first keeper to man the light was William D. Jones. No dwelling was erected when the mast was constructed, so Jones took it upon himself to build his own dwelling. With nearby driftwood, he constructed what would become his longtime home.

Despite the light guiding large shipping vessels, tragedy still struck. Jones' diary tells of saving a sailor's life from the choppy waters, only to watch him die from the shock. That was in 1905. A year later two boats collided, tearing apart one and trapping eight people inside the other. The tug with the eight people sank, their remains still trapped inside on the ocean floor today. Despite these tragedies, William D. Jones remained at his post as lighthouse keeper until he was 81. Today the lighthouse is operated under the care of the Vancouver Parks and Recreation Board.

BELOW & RIGHT: Brockton Point Lighthouse was designed and built in 1914 by Colonel William Anderson.

HOW TO GET THERE

The lighthouse grounds are open to the public. To get there, take BC-99/Seymour Street. Make a left onto W Georgia St/BC-1A/BC-99. Turn right onto Stanley Park Road, then make a left onto Stanley Park Drive. Mind the fork and stay left as you continue on Stanley Park Drive toward the lighthouse.

Address
Stanley Park
Vancouver, BC V6G 3E2

CAPE BONAVISTA LIGHT

Built: 1843
Style: House-style, Wooden
Height: 36 feet (10.97m)

Unique because of its style and candy-striped colors on the house and lighthouse tower, this North American light in Canada was built to mark the entrance of Trinity and Bonavista Bays. The light functioned from 1843 until 1966 when it became automated. During its heyday, it served thousands of mariners who used the waterways for shipping goods.

The Newfoundland government recognized the need for the light in 1841. After surveying the site and appropriating funds it was determined that the site was sound and construction could begin. The much-anticipated light was built with a design based on the Trinity House in England. A rotating red and white light, originally used in the Bell Rock Lighthouse, was installed inside the lantern room. After several months of delay due to some issues with construction, the light was finally lit for the first time in September of 1843. The light was deactivated in 1966.

Much later in 2001, lightning would strike the tower, causing it to catch on fire. Thanks to a quick response team, however, there would be limited damage. The antique light was not affected during the fire because it was off-site at the time for repairs.

The steel tower next to the colorful structure lights the way for mariners today. The original lighthouse is now the Newfoundland Provincial Historic Museum. Visitors also go to the area to try and catch a glimpse of whales or puffins. The waterways are also known for their icebergs.

BELOW & RIGHT: In 2001 a disastrous electrical storm struck Cape Bonavista. As lightning struck repeatedly all around the cape, the lighthouse tower was hit three times, igniting a fire. Quick action by the fire department prevented more severe damage.

HOW TO GET THERE

The lighthouse is open to the public from May to October with guided tours. Take the Port aux Basques Ferry to Newfoundland. Once there, take TC-1 E. Merge onto NL-230 from exit 26 towards Catalina/Bonavista. NL-230 becomes Confederation Drive. Make a left to continue on Confederation Drive. After a mile, turn right onto Cape Shore Road.

Address
505 Cape Shore Rd.
Bonavista
NL A0C 1B0

CAPE SPEAR LIGHT

Built: 1836
Style: House-Style, Wooden
Height: 36 feet (10.97m)

HOW TO GET THERE

The lighthouse is open to the public. To visit, take exit 41A and merge onto NL-2 E toward Mount Pearl. After fifteen miles, turn right onto Hamilton Ave. Make a sharp right onto Water Street, then a left onto Blackhead Road.

Address
Blackhead Rd.
St. John's
NL A1C 5H2

It seems that the colors red and white don most of the lighthouses along the waterways of Canada. Situated on the busy eastern point of North America, this sprawling lighthouse with several additions was the ideal place to erect a beacon. Some believe the light was named Cape Spear (French for hope) because sailors likely felt hope when they finally saw land after being away from home for so long.

The oldest standing lighthouse in the province, the two-story wooden structure was finished in 1835 but wasn't lit until the following year when the light arrived. The beacon was illuminated by whale oil and used seven wicks surrounded by reflectors to create a flash of light every sixty seconds.

Roughly ten years after it was built, Prince Henry of the Netherlands was expected to visit. As the people waited for his ship to dock, concern grew when the *Rhine* didn't show. Several men, including a local man named James Cantwell, oared out onto the water in search of the ship. Cantwell saw the lost vessel on the water and climbed aboard to steer it back to shore. Pleased with what Cantwell had done, the Prince asked him how he could repay him. Cantwell said, "I would like to be the lightkeeper at Cape Spear." Not only was he made lighthouse keeper, Prince Henry made sure that the post would be manned by the Cantwell family thereafter, too. The Cantwell family was large. Soon, a young woman by the name of Margaret Hefferan took a job on site as a teacher to help educate the eight children of the Cantwell brothers. She ended up marrying one of them, and they had children of their own. The Cantwell family tenure ended with the last Cantwell leaving his post for good in 1997.

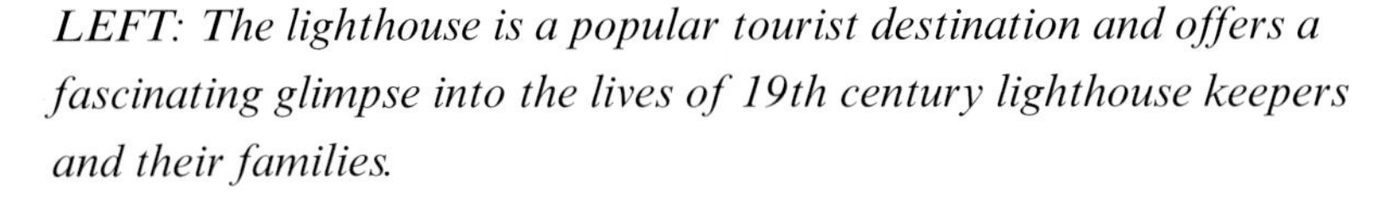

LEFT: The lighthouse is a popular tourist destination and offers a fascinating glimpse into the lives of 19th century lighthouse keepers and their families.

COVE ISLAND LIGHT

Built: 1858
Style: Imperial, Stone
Height: 80 feet (24.38m)

The Cove Island Light at Gig Point on Bruce Peninsula is a favorite among locals. This tall, brick structure has been guiding ships by marking the passage between Georgian Bay and Lake Huron for years. Painted white with red features, it can't be missed on a clear day along the water.

While it is located inside of Fathom Five National Marine Park, it is not actually part of the park. Before it was an iconic lighthouse station, the area was lit only by a series of lamps raised on poles. When the Imperial Government recognized the growth of mass transportation both on the railway and waterway, they appropriated funds to construct a series of lighthouses along the shoreline.

Construction on the lighthouse began in 1855 and took about four years. White limestone was dragged to the site by horse so that over two dozen men could assemble the tower. At times, construction was delayed due to budgetary reasons. The Fresnel lens didn't even make it to the site

until October of 1858. When it was finally assembled and lit, it was described by the engineer as a "brilliant flame that illuminates the whole horizon."

Life was difficult on the remote island. One lighthouse keeper by the name of David McBeath, nearly starved to death with his wife and five children. It was cold on the island, and food rations were gone. The keeper sent letters, begging for help. Each ship on the water received the pleas, but only one letter was able to get through. A steamer called the *Rescue* made it to the island just in time to see the family leaving the island during a storm on a raft.

Today, the original buildings and lighthouse still stand on the island. The light is used as a navigational aid and blinks a white light from the top every five seconds.

BELOW LEFT & BELOW: Pictured below are the lighthouse tower, the original house and fog plant, a workshop, the assistant keeper's house, and the modern lightkeeper's house.

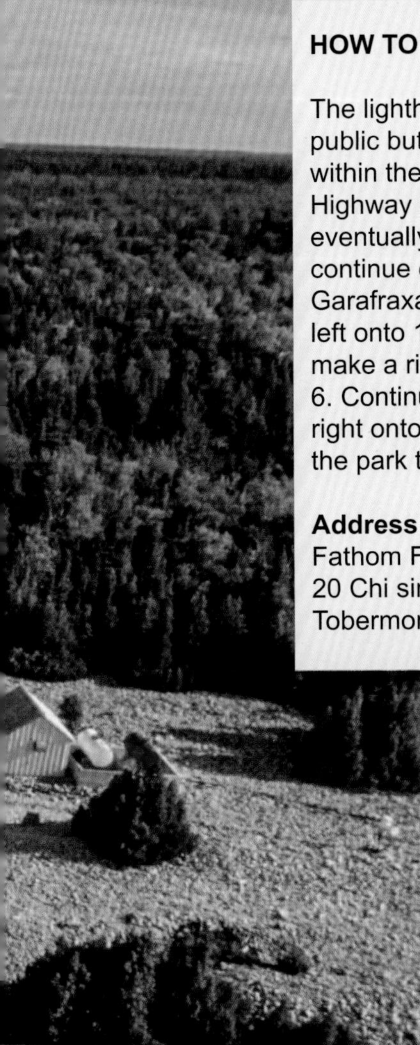

HOW TO GET THERE

The lighthouse is closed to the public but can still be viewed from within the park. To get there, take Highway 89/ON-89/ON-10, eventually making a right to continue on it. Turn right onto Garafraxa Street, and then make a left onto 10th Street. From here, make a right onto Highway 6/ON-6. Continue to follow ON-6. Turn right onto Front St. Continue into the park to reach the lighthouse.

Address
Fathom Five National Marine Park
20 Chi sin tib dek Rd.
Tobermory, ON N0H 2R0

FISGARD LIGHT

Built: 1860
Style: Cylindrical, Brick
Height: 56 feet (17.06m)

This historic light was originally constructed by the British before Vancouver Island was owned by Canada, and was British Columbia's first official lighthouse. The brick for the tower was shipped from Great Britain. Like many other Canadian Imperial lights, the building of the tower was funded by the British Empire's Board of Trade. It stands graciously at the entrance of Esquimalt Harbour, marking the home base of the Royal Canadian Navy.

The lighthouse keeper's home is a Victoria-style dwelling and was built soundly on the foundation of granite brick, some two feet thick. Surrounding the light station is a brick wall topped with granite slab. The dwelling itself is two-stories and offers rooms on each floor that are quite spacious. The staircase inside was built in California and spirals upward to the lantern room.

The keepers at Fisgard were poorly paid and didn't man their posts very long. This was not because of the lowly pay–they either died of illness or drowned. After the last keeper left in 1929, the lighthouse fell into shambles, and some of the logbooks inside were destroyed. It wasn't until the early 1980s that Parks Canada restored the lighthouse and dwelling to its original state, turning part of it into a museum. The light at the top, which was officially automated in 1929, is still active today and flashes a red and white light every two seconds toward Victoria.

BELOW & RIGHT: Inside the building are two floors of exhibits dealing with shipwrecks, storms, far-flung lights, and the everyday working equipment of the lightkeeper a century ago.

HOW TO GET THERE

The lighthouse is open to the public. To enjoy its beauty, and perhaps take in a picnic, head north on Douglas Street until it becomes Highway 1. Continue on 1 for 5 km to Colwood exit 10. Follow Highway 1A for 2 km and then turn left at the third traffic light onto Ocean Boulevard. From here, follow the signs to the lighthouse.

Address
603 Fort Rodd Hill Rd.
Victoria, BC V9C 2W8

UNDER-WATER-CABLE

GEORGES ISLAND LIGHT

HOW TO GET THERE

The lighthouse is not open to the public but can be viewed from the pier. To reach the pier, take Barrington Street/NS-2 until it becomes Hollis Sreett. Turn left onto Terminal Road. Terminal Road becomes Marginal Road (Gate access required). Turn right to stay on Marginal Road.

Address
Canadian Museum of Immigration at Pier 21
1055 Marginal Rd.
Halifax, NS B3H 4P7

Built: 1917
Style: Octagonal, Concrete
Height: 58 feet (17.67m)

In the mid-nineteenth century, Halifax, Nova Scotia, was fast becoming a bustling harbor and port. New York experienced a massive influx of immigrants at this time, and so did Halifax, taking in almost 95,000 people in 1913. Between the exploding population and the transit of mass goods, the harbor was in high demand. The only light at the Halifax Harbour at the time was the Chebucto Head Light. On the breakwater nearby was Maugher Beach Light. To improve visibility, Georges Island light was added to the mix in 1876.

In 1916, a fire destroyed the lighthouse, burning it to the ground. Until a new one could be erected, a makeshift tower was put up to continue in aiding navigation. The following year, the current lighthouse was constructed. The iconic red stripe on the tower was added in 1973. The light at the top flashed green until 1977. It was fully automated in 1992, but the future of the lighthouse was uncertain.

Considered part of the Halifax Harbour Inner Range, the light today is under the ownership of Parks Canada. It is still used as a navigational aid, but now blinks a white, flashing light. The hope is that the lighthouse will soon be open for a full viewing and historic tour. It can be seen from the Canadian Museum of Immigration at Pier 21.

LEFT & BELOW: This light can easily be seen from the Halifax Harbour Front.

GIBRALTAR POINT LIGHT

Built: 1808
Style: Hexagonal, Stone

Gibraltar Point Light is considered the oldest standing lighthouse on the Great Lakes. This particular point was named in 1793 when the first Lieutenant Governor of Upper Canada decided to move the capital of the province to Toronto (then York) where he felt it was less prone to attack. The point is long and finger-like, creating a natural peninsula into Lake Ontario. To protect it, the Lt. Governor ordered that Fort York be constructed. He felt it couldn't be conquered, and aptly named the point Gibraltar Point to reflect its strength. Later in 1803, it was determined that the area needed further protection, as did the vessels that traveled along the water. This is when Parliament agreed to the construction of three lighthouses: Gibraltar Point, Mississauga Point, and Nine Mile Point.

While many lighthouses have ghost stories as part of their history, the Gibraltar Point light is probably best known for its own haunted tale. The story goes that the first lighthouse keeper to man the tower was murdered. His name was John Paul Radelmüller, and it is said that two drunken soldiers, in search of more alcohol that Radelmüller concocted himself, climbed the tower one night and murdered him. To try and hide the crime, they chopped up his remains and attempted to bury them in gravesites nearby. The story is told during school trips and tours, adding that the former lighthouse keeper can be seen wandering the grounds and flashing lights where no lights actually exist.

Today, just about every single lighthouse in North America is automated and no longer manned. This lighthouse, however, still has a keeper on duty. He has been the honorary keeper since 1999, and continues to keep the lighthouse in working order to preserve its history and natural beauty. The lighthouse is owned by the city of Toronto. Tours are available by appointment.

BELOW & RIGHT: Gibraltar Light is one of many which are said to be haunted. In this particular case the hauntings are by the first lighthouse keeper, John Paul Radelmüller who ho was murdered in 1815.

HOW TO GET THERE

To reach the Lighthouse on Centre Island, take the ferry across from the Mainland Ferry Docks to either Centre Island, Ward's Island, or Hanlan's Point. Once on land, visitors have over a mile to walk to the lighthouse.

Address
443 Lakeshore Ave.
Toronto, ON M5J 2W2

LOUISBOURG LIGHT

Built: 1923
Style: Octagonal, Concrete
Height: 55 feet (16.76m)

This underappreciated lighthouse once greeted hundreds of vessels coming into Louisbourg Harbor on the foggiest of nights. This lonely beacon is Canada's oldest light station, and can only be accessed via a well-groomed trail. It is the third tower to be built on this site. The first was built in 1729 after the *Le Profound*, one of the ships of the King's fleet, met its demise on the rocks at the end of the harbor. At the time, only a bonfire warned mariners of the turbulent rocks. It is unclear if a fire was lit on this particular night.

To stop any more shipwrecks, construction of the first tower started in 1731. It was a circular tower made of rubble stone. The lanterns for the light didn't arrive until 1734. Cod oil lit the lamps, which could be seen for eighteen nautical miles. Despite its strong illumination, it was prone to catching fire, and did so in 1736. The tower itself was unaffected, but the light had to be rebuilt. It held steady until the second British siege of Louisbourg when the tower was seriously damaged during battle in 1758.

The second lighthouse was built in 1842 as a keeper's dwelling with the lantern room protruding from the top. Fire destroyed it completely in 1922. The third tower was constructed the following year and still stands today, guarding the waters. The Louisbourg Lighthouse Society is working hard to bring more attention to the historic structure. While the interior of the lighthouse itself is not open for viewing, the light itself is fully operational and can be seen from the trail.

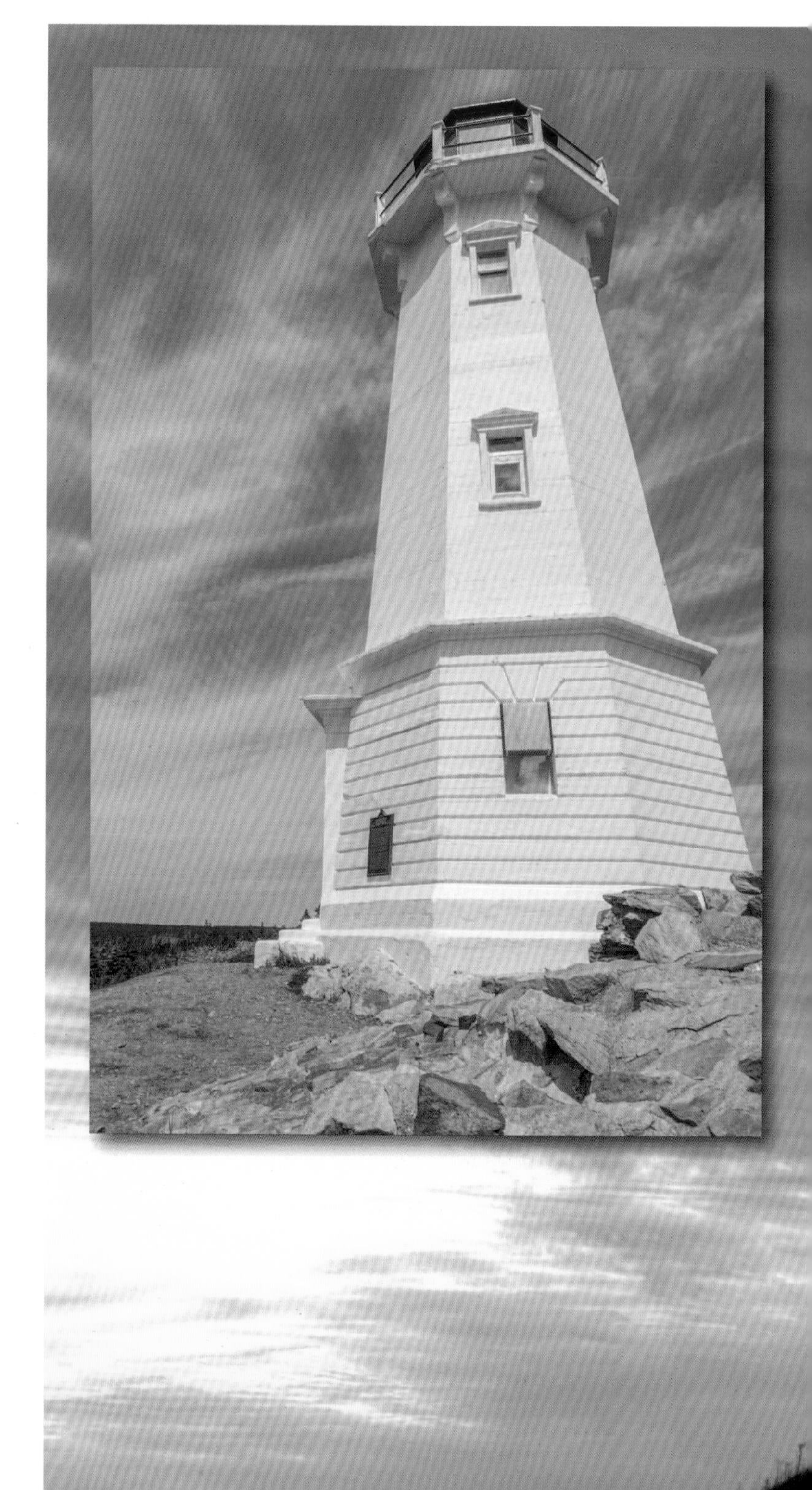

RIGHT: This historic site, where Canada's first lighthouse was first lit in 1734, offers one of the most picturesque coastal vistas in Nova Scotia.

HOW TO GET THERE

Follow the clearly marked trail to the lighthouse for just over a mile. To reach the trail, take the NS-125 E ramp toward Louisbourg and then merge onto Highway 125/NS-125. Take NS-22 exit 8 toward George Street. Enter the next roundabout and take the first exit onto Louisbourg Highway/NS-22. Louisbourg Highway/NS-22 becomes Main Street. From Main, make a left onto Havenside Road.

Address
555 Havenside Rd.
Louisbourg, NS B1C 1PA

MARGARETSVILLE LIGHT

Built: 1859
Style: Tapered Square, Wood
Height: 22 feet (6.7m)

It took the residents of Margaretsville to convince officials that a lighthouse was needed to guide vessels in the right direction on the Bay of Fundy. At the time, only about six lighthouses lit up the shoreline. When it was built in 1859, it proved worthy, and still stands today reminding visitors of its strength.

While some lights used whale or cod oil, this light used kerosene. Logs kept by the keepers showed that up to twelve gallons were used per month. The wicks were lit at sunset and put out when the sun started to rise. These wicks were powered by eight large lamps with brass reflectors and had to be cleaned and filled with kerosene daily. The first keeper to maintain the wicks was William Early. After he passed, he was replaced by his son, John Early, who traveled far and wide with his wife to get to the site, and worked hard to maintain the beacon. When he died, his wife Ruth took the post and is said to be the first and only woman to keep the light at Margaretsville.

The year she took the massive lighthouse keeper duties over, was the same year that the kerosene lantern was removed and replaced with a cast iron top. It is the same one that is in use on the tower today. The light continues to guide mariners along the Bay of Fundy. It is also part of a redevelopment plan to improve the sights and historic pieces of the Margaretsville waterfront.

HOW TO GET THERE

To reach the light, take Highway 101 to Annapolis Valley to Exit 18A toward Spa Springs. Make a right and then left onto Highway 362. Follow Highway 362 up North Mountain to Margaretsville on the coast. Watch for lighthouse signs and follow the signs.

Address
Lighthouse Rd.
Margaretsville, NS B0S 1N0

RIGHT: The black-and-white 22-foot Margaretsville Lighthouse figures prominently in the history of Canadian navigation lights.

North Point
Lightstation
Phare de
la pointe Nord
Canada

NORTH CAPE LIGHT

Built: 1865
Style: Octagonal
Height: 64 feet (19.5m)

HOW TO GET THERE

The lighthouse is not open to the public but can be seen from the North Cape Wind Energy Interpretive Centre. To get to the centre, take Highway 10/PE-10. Turn left onto Route 1A/PE-1A. After six miles, enter a roundabout and take the 2nd exit onto PE-2. Pass through two more roundabouts. Make a left onto Church St/PE-14. Take the 1st right onto Dalton Avenue, and then left onto Conroy Road/PE-12. Continue to follow to Route 12.

Address
North Cape Wind Energy Interpretive Centre
21817 Route 12
North Cape, Tignish
PE C0B 2B0

The long reef that extends from the tip of Prince Edward Island for well over a mile delves into the space that divides with earnest the Gulf of St. Lawrence and the Northumberland Strait. As ships passed by this area, it was with great uncertainty, especially in the dark. So when a report that was issued in 1834 addressing the necessity of a light went ignored, ship owners upped the ante by circulating a petition. The petition was presented to the House of Assembly of Prince Edward Island in 1840. This entity reached out to the Imperial Government and US officials, asking for financial assistance.

For decades, the request was ignored. None of the governments of the Canadian colonies or the US could decide what amount to contribute was fair. In 1861, one frustrated mariner placed a makeshift light at the site. Still, higher officials ignored the need for a lighthouse and station, even after several shipwrecks had been logged. After more requests and petitions, the tower was finally erected in 1865.

The lighthouse proved to be a very useful beacon on North Cape, and when the light wasn't deemed bright enough, it was replaced with a bigger one in 1875. For years the light station operated with success until 1945, when engineers noticed the keeper's home needed to be moved away from the cliff. But, like the lighthouse's own slow beginning, the move never happened and the dwelling fell into awful disrepair. Ice from the waters below destroyed it, forcing one keeper to have to chop his way out after a massive storm that froze the doors and windows shut. Today the lighthouse is automated and attracts tourists from all over the country. It is owned by Parks Canada.

LEFT: The lighthouse is still active and is operated by the Canadian Coast Guard. It is closed to the public.

185

HOW TO GET THERE

The lighthouse is only an hour from Halifax. To get there, take Highway 333 from Halifax or Highway 103 from Halifax to Exit 5. From here, continue along Route 333 to Peggy's Point Road.

Address
Peggy's Point Rd.
Peggy's Cove
NS B3Z 3R9

PEGGY'S COVE LIGHT

Built: 1915
Style: Octagonal, Concrete
Height: 50 feet (15.25m)

If you've ever gone to a post office to get your mail, it was likely not at a tall, white and red lighthouse. However, such is not the case at Peggy's Cove Light. Built on granite ledges that are estimated to be some 400 million years old just southwest of Halifax, this monument that was finished one year after the Confederation of Canada was formed, is now larger than life. Not only does it double as a post office, but it is still an active aid to navigation and a hotspot for tourists and photographers alike.

How the lighthouse earned the name Peggy's Cove is not clear. Some say it's short for Margaret, and aptly named because of nearby Saint Margaret's Bay. Others follow the lore of a woman named Peggy who was the only survivor of a shipwreck in the cove. The first light that was built on the site was wood and built in 1868. The present light was erected on the ancient rock in 1915.

Visitors of the lighthouse should look along the rock for etchings. On one of the granite stones are figures of fishermen, their families, and the lighthouse. There's no telling who or when the etchings were made, but it is clear it was done in the early days of the lighthouse. The light was automated in 1958. Today, it features a fixed, red light and is managed by the Canadian Coast Guard.

LEFT & BELOW: Peggy's Cove is famed for its picturesque and typically East-Coast profile, with houses perched along a narrow inlet and on wave-washed boulders facing the Atlantic. Although this unique environment has been designated a preservation area, it is still an active fishing community.

POINT ATKINSON LIGHT

Built: 1912
Style: Conical, Concrete
Height: 60 feet (18.28m)

Located in southern British Columbia, life at the Point Atkinson Light wasn't easy. Walter Erwin was the first lightkeeper to take his post there. From 1880 to 1910, he and his family dutifully managed the tower and the bright beacon above. He was paid $700 a year, plenty to raise his family on. But when the station was upgraded with a foghorn in 1889, his pay was cut in half so that he could pay an assistant to man the horn. The family struggled, and often fell ill due to work-related illnesses. However, they soldiered on until the day Erwin retired, with a meager $33-a-month pension.

Before Walter Erwin stepped foot on the rocky bluff, the first tower was erected. It was 1875, and the beacon attached to a keeper's dwelling was made of wood. After Erwin left, the assistant who absorbed half of Erwin's pay took over. His name was Thomas Grafton, and he took in the likes of the new 1912 tower and dwelling that was constructed beside it.

A few other keepers rotated manning the station over the next several years until Gerald Watson took the post over in 1980. An educated university man and historian, Watson wrote two books on the life of a keeper in British Columbia. He has since passed, but today his wife Elaine spearheads the West Vancouver Historical Society's Point Atkinson Light Station subcommittee. Her mission is to secure funding to further restore the iconic lighthouse.

HOW TO GET THERE

Heading toward West Vancouver, take Headland Drive and turn left onto Westport Road, then left onto Caulfeild Drive. Make another left onto Willow Creek Road, and then a slight left onto Keith Road. From here, turn right onto Marine Drive. Be prepared to make a sharp left onto The Dale. Next, take the 2nd right onto Water Lane. make a left onto Beacon Lane.

Address
Lighthouse Park
4902 Beacon Lane
West Vancouver, BC V7W 1K5

RIGHT: Point Atkinson Lighthouse can be reached by hiking the Valley Trail in Lighthouse Park.

POINT CLARK LIGHT

Built: 1859
Style: Imperial, Limestone
Height: 80 feet (24.38m)

It started as a lantern hung on a pine tree at the point, about 18 kilometers sound of Kincardine, and turned into one of six lighthouses authorized by the Province of Canada known as the Imperial towers. The six beacons were part of an "illuminated wall" that would aid sailors along Lake Huron and Georgian Bay. This particular tower was necessary to alert sailors of an offshore shoal and reef jutting out into the point.

Originally called Pine Point, the lighthouse station's first keeper was John Young, a 55-year-old laborer who would manage the site until 1882. He was responsible for keeping the wicks burning, cleaning the lens, and winding up the mechanism that turned the lens. Of course, this was just the beginning of his duties. The life of a lighthouse keeper went far beyond managing the lantern room.

Point Clark saw a handful of lighthouse keepers move through its doors, including George Ray, who was the last to keep watch until the light was automated in 1924. However, mariners claimed the automated light wasn't bright enough, and another keeper was brought in to resume duties in 1926. It would remain traditionally kept until 1962 when it was automated again. The lighthouse has since been restored, and after a $1.7 million dollar contract was awarded to aid in the restoration, the lighthouse was opened to the public in 2015.

BELOW & RIGHT: The keeper's cottage is an important place of historic interest. It is listed on the Canadian Register of Historic Places.

HOW TO GET THERE

The lighthouse is open to the public from June until Labor Day. To get there, take Britannia Road E/ON-21. Take the first right onto Victoria Street. Continue to follow Victoria street until it's time to make a left onto Concession Road After nearly three miles, turn left onto Huron Road, then right onto Lighthouse Road.

Address
530 Lighthouse Rd.
Point Clark, ON N0G 2R0

HOW TO GET THERE

The lighthouse is open to the public June through September. To get there, take TC-16 E until it becomes TC-1 E. Enter the roundabout and take the first exit to Capital Drive. Turn right onto University Avenue. University Avenue becomes Great George Street. From here, turn left onto Grafton Street. Grafton Street becomes TC-1 E. Turn right onto Point Prim Road and park in the lighthouse parking lot.

Address
2147 Point Prim Rd.
Belfast, PE COA 1AO

POINT PRIM LIGHT

Built: 1845
Style: Conical, Brick
Height: 60 feet (18.28m)

As the oldest lighthouse on Prince Edward Island, this conical structure was an uninvited idea for roughly three years before officials could decide on appropriate funding and an ideal location. Starting in 1841, shipowners were adamant with the colony's House of Assembly, citing the need after sharing the number of shipwrecks logged at the harbour entrance at Charlottetown. When officials finally gave in, it was barely enough to cover the cost of materials. As a result, work was stalled.

Sometime in 1844, leaders of the Steam Navigation Company on the island stepped up, complaining about the lack of lights on the waterway. Area merchants also chimed in, citing their loyalty and financial contributions to the colony. Finally, the land was surveyed and a suitable contractor was hired. The light came to life for the first time in December of 1845. The first keeper to light the wicks was John Ings, and he accepted an annual salary of £50, which is $58.31 in American dollars. With no keeper's dwelling for residency, Ings was forced to make his one on the second floor of the lighthouse. A cottage was built some years later.

Visitors can explore the lighthouse and the grounds, including the keeper's cottage that was renovated in 2017, and now acts as a museum and storefront.

LEFT & ABOVE: The keeper's cottage was renovated in 2017. It sells gifts and houses exhibitions.

ROSE BLANCHE LIGHT

Built: 1873
Style: House-style, Granite
Height: 40 feet (12.19m)

White quartz rocks are signature at Rose Blanche Light, and are likely a part of how the site got its name. In French, rose blanche means white rose. And while no roses don the site where the lighthouse sits, plenty of the quartz rocks do, making this light station unique in its own right.

The beacon and keeper's dwelling are one, which is a common style for many lighthouses. In this particular structure, the stove in the kitchen was built too close to the granite walls, causing it to be extremely hot in the summer. To remedy the situation a new, separate kitchen was built outside, doubling as a porch. Sometime in 1890 it was noted that the solid granite lighthouse and dwelling were difficult to see in the daytime because it blended in with the granite rocks on the point. To help mariners better see the station, the two sides of the dwelling facing the water were painted with red and white stripes.

Most notable about Rose Blanche is that at one point in the early 20th century, fifteen children and three adults made this little lighthouse their home. Keeper John Cook married a widow with three children, and together they had six more. Soon, her sister moved in with six of her own. Cook, the keeper of the light, had to build an addition on the dwelling to accommodate his large family. Today, the dwelling is still home to many a family, as it is a popular stop for those visiting the area.

HOW TO GET THERE

The Rose Blanche Light is open to the public from June to September, and sits on the southwest coast of Newfoundland. Take Route 470 for about 28 miles to the Marine Atlantic Ferry terminal in Port Aux Basques. When exiting the ferry, the ramp to Route 470 is on the right. Take 470 to Water Bottom Road.

Address
75 Water Bottom Road
Rose Blanche-Harbour le Cou
NL A0M 1P0

RIGHT: Rose Blanche Light is accessed by a gravel trail that showcases spectacular views of the lighthouse, ocean, and harbor. The original lighthouse was built in 1873 to mark the entrance to the harbor. It is known locally as the Cains Island Lighthouse.

SEAL ISLAND LIGHT

Built: 1985
Style: Octagonal, Wood
Height: 35 feet (10.66m)

This particular red and white striped light is actually a museum and replica of the top part of the original light that was built here in 1831. The cast iron light is original, and is iconic to the Barrington community. In 1978, the light was removed so that it could be shipped to the National Museum of Science and Technology in Ottawa. However, thanks to locals advocating for the preservation of the light, it was helicoptered back and brought to Barrington. Being the only Fresnel Lens installed in any of the lighthouses throughout Nova Scotia, residents felt strongly about keeping at home. Their voices were heard. The antique lens now sits atop the replica lighthouse, along with the original clockwork mechanism, for visitors to see.

"We are told to let our light shine, and if it does, we won't need to tell anybody it does. Lighthouses don't fire cannons to call attention to their shining–they just shine."

Dwight L. Moody

HOW TO GET THERE

The museum is open to the public June through September. There is a fee to enter. You can reach the replica by taking NS-213 ramp toward Hammonds Plains Road. Turn left onto Hammonds Plains Road. Merge onto NS-103 W toward Hubbards/Yarmouth, and then make a left onto NS-3/Highway 3.

Address
2422 Highway 3
Barrington NS B0W 1E0

LEFT & RIGHT: Inside the museum are numerous artifacts from the local area chronicling the lives of local lighthouse keepers and the area's rich seafaring history. The museum houses the second order Fresnel lens, which was in use from 1902 to 1978 in the Seal Island Lighthouse. A panoramic view of Barrington Bay is visible from the top of the lighthouse museum.

SWALLOWTAIL LIGHT

Built: 1860
Style: Wooden
Height: 53 feet (16.15m)

This iconic wooden tower was the third of nine structures built in the Grand Manan islands, and sits comfortably at the entrance of North Head Harbour. The light was deemed necessary after the 1857 shipwreck of the Lord Ashburton, which took the lives of over twenty seamen. A handful survived, including a sailor by the name of James Lawson.

After the massive ship grounded on the shore of Grand Manan in the early morning hours, Lawson stumbled onto land until he found a barn where he collapsed. It was January, and winter was no friend to the sailors. Later that day he was discovered, along with seven other men scattered about in the area. Lawson was badly injured, and had to have his feet amputated. For five years he recovered in a hospital. When he left, he worked as a shoemaker and settled down into married life. By then, the Swallowtail Light had been erected and was in full service.

Lawson's tragedy wasn't the first and it wouldn't be the last. Years later, a lighthouse keeper's wife died after overfilling the burners. The lantern room burst into flames, catching her dress on fire. She raced down the stairs and was aided by her son, but later died from the burns. The boy was able to extinguish the flames in the lantern room before fire spread throughout the tower. Today, those stories are part of a tour offered by the Swallowtail Keepers Society, who has a long-term lease on the property. The light is still an active aid to navigation today.

BELOW & RIGHT: Swallowtail Lighthouse and the surrounding buildings and peninsula are owned by the Village of Grand Manan and managed by the Swallowtail Keepers Society.

HOW TO GET THERE

From New Brunswick, head southwest on Digby Ferry Road. It will turn into Lancaster Street. From here, make a right onto Saint John Street. Turn left onto Market Place. Be prepared to merge onto the Saint John Throughway. Then merge onto Main Street toward Saint John Centre. Turn left onto Union Street and then right onto Germain Street.

Address
Grand Manan Island
NB E5G 2A3

WESTERN HEAD LIGHT

Built: 1962
Style: Octagonal, Concrete
Height: 40 feet (12.19m)

The Western Head Light began as a foghorn station. Built in 1924, the station was considered enough for navigation. Erected near Liverpool Bay, the loud horn certainly aided mariners, but simply wasn't enough as the waterways became more populated with shipping vessels. Therefore, to assist with navigation, the current tower was erected in 1962.

As one of the youngest towers in Nova Scotia, maintenance on both the tower and fog horn was pertinent. The foghorn alone had to be monitored regularly in the winter months to keep it clear of relentless ice and snow. In the tower, the lens had to be polished and cleared of ice regularly as well.

Today, the tower serves as a weather station for Environment Canada. The light itself was unmanned in 1988 when it became automated. The red lantern at the top offers a flashing white light to ships below and is still used as a navigational aid today.

BELOW & RIGHT: As indicated by its name, the lighthouse is situated along the western approach to Liverpool Bay, while Coffin Island Lighthouse marks the eastern approaches.

HOW TO GET THERE

Take northeast on Highway 3/NS-3 toward River Road. Turn right onto River Road. Make a sharp left onto Little Harbour Road until you reach Lighthouse Road.

Address
141 Lighthouse Rd.
Western Head, NS B0T 1K0

WOOD ISLANDS RANGE LIGHTS

WOOD ISLANDS FRONT RANGE LIGHT

Built: 1962
Style: Octagonal, Concrete
Height: 40 feet (12.19m)

The first of the Wood Island Lights, this keeper's dwelling was constructed with a beacon atop it that originally held a Fresnel lens with a fixed, white light. It was constructed with materials dredged from the harbor. The site itself was quite isolated until a road was built sometime in 1940. This allowed keepers to travel and gather with ease to purchase much-needed goods. Prior to this, the keeper and his family had to rely on a rowboat to reach populated land.

In 1941 a fog horn building was added to the site to aid with the much anticipated new ferry service. Sometime in the 1980s, the Canadian

HOW TO GET THERE

Both lights can be found on the southeastern shore of Prince Edward Island. From the ferry in Caribou, take Highway 1 from Charlottetown on Prince Edward Island to Wood Islands. Near the ferry landing, take Lighthouse Road east to the Wood Islands Lighthouse site.

Address
173 Lighthouse Rd.
Belle River, PE C0A 1B0

Coast Guard had a new dwelling built for the last lighthouse keeper, with the intention to tear the old dwelling and lighthouse down. But locals protested, and the historic lighthouse was preserved instead. The newer dwelling was removed from the site in 1991. In 2009, the first lighthouse was moved away from the edge of the bank and relocated about 150 meters from shore. The lighthouse is now a gift shop and open to the public for tours.

WOOD ISLANDS BACK RANGE LIGHT

Built: 1902
Style: Pyramidal, Wooden
Height: 32 feet (9.75m)

This lighthouse faces seaward and stands without a keeper's dwelling. It was constructed in 1902 to overlook the Northumberland Strait leading toward Wood Islands Harbour. In its early days it had a red stripe painted down the side, but it was removed when the light was decommissioned in 2007.

After it was built, keeper James Young was the first lighthouse keeper to manage the range lights, both front and back. He served until 1935 when he resigned. This light was also moved to avoid erosion, but it was relocated much earlier than the first. In 1941, officials did the work to move the light to the pier west of the first light. It was moved again in 2013 so that it would be closer to the first Wood Islands Lighthouse.

LEFT: Wood Islands Front Range Light.

BELOW: Wood Islands Back Range Light with the Front Light in the background.

Index

Entries in capitals are lighthouses featured in this book

A
Acadia National Park 54
Adam, John Quincy 82
Alaska Panhandle 176
ALCATRAZ ISLAND LIGHT 164
Alcona Historical Society 47
Alice Wellington Rollins 22
ALKI POINT LIGHT 167
Anglin, Clarence 164
Annisquam Harbor 52
ANNISQUAM HARBOR LIGHT 52
Argand, Froncois Pierre Ami 10
Aristotle 151
Armour, Captain James A 143
Army Corp of Engineers 93, 174
Assateague Island 108
ASSATEAGUE LIGHTHOUSE 108
Augusta 28

B
BACCARO POINT LIGHT 210
Baddeck HARBOUR/Kidston Island Light 213
Baltimore Maritime Museum 152
Barrington Bay 210
Barrows Island Light 184
Bass Harbor 54
BASS HARBOR HEAD LIGHT 54
Bass Islands 34
Battery Point 168
BATTERY POINT (CRESCENT CITY) LIGHT 168
Bay of Fundy 215, 232
Bell, Alexander Graham 213
Blackbeard, pirate 148
Black Lake 30
BILOXI LIGHT 110
Blue Hill Bay 54
Bodie Island Lights 124
Boothbay Harbor, Maine 68
Boston Harbor, Massachusetts
Boston Light 8
BRANT POINT LIGHT 56
BRIER ISLAND LIGHT 214
British Columbia 216, 238
British Empire's Board of Trade 224
Bristol Parks Commission 83
BROCKTON POINT LIGHT 216
Buzzard's Bay 80

C
Cabrillo National Monument 190
California State Coastal Conservancy 196
Calvert Maritime Museum. 126
Canadian Coast Guard 237, 253
Canadian Imperial lights 224
Canadian Museum of Immigration 227
Canadian Register of Historic Places 240
Cantwell, James 221
Cape Argo 180
CAPE BLANCO LIGHT 170
CAPE BONAVISTA LIGHT 218
Cape Breton Highlands 213
Cape Canaveral 150
Cape Cod 60, 78
Cape Florida 136
CAPE FLORIDA LIGHT 112
Cape Foulweather 180, 206
CAPE HATTERAS LIGHT 114
Cape Hatteras Lights 124
Cape Hatteras National Seashore 114
Cape Henry 124
CAPE HENRY LIGHTS 146
Cape Lookout 172
CAPE LOOKOUT LIGHT 117
Cape Lookout National Seashore 117
CAPE MEARES LIGHT 172
CAPE NEDDICK LIGHT 58
CAPE SAN BLAS LIGHT 118
CAPE SPEAR LIGHT 221
Carysfort Reef 112
Cattle Point Light 184
Cedar Point Light 17
Chappaquiddick Island 64
Charlotte, Layton 200
Charlottetown 243
Chatham 78
CHATHAM LIGHT 60
Chebucto Head light 227
Chesapeake Bay 108, 122, 138, 146, 152
Chicago Harbor Light 18
Chicago River 19
Chincoteague National Wildlife Refuge 108
Chinook Pier 25
Choragic Monument of Lysicrates 84
City of Bangor 21
Clara Nevada, steamer 176
COCKSPUR ISLAND LIGHT 121
Coffin Island Lighthouse 250
Columbian Exposition 43
CONCORD POINT LIGHT 122
Connecticut River 94
Conro, Isaac 96
Cook, John 244
COQUILLE RIVER LIGHT 174
COVE ISLAND LIGHT 222
Cray, Captain Robert 179
Cumberland County, New Jersey 62
CURRITUCK BEACH LIGHT 124

D
Dagget, Peter 80
Dalén, Nils Gustaf 12
Daniel R. Platt 44
Del Norte County Historical Society 168
Dickens, Charles 128
Digby Neck 215
Delaware Bay 62
Dolphin, schooner 48
DRUM POINT LIGHT 126
DRY TORTUGAS LIGHT 128, 130
Dry Tortugas National Park 130
Dungeness Point 188
Dungeness Spit 188

E
Eagle Harbor Light 20
Early, John 232
Early, William 232
EAST POINT LIGHT 62
EDGARTOWN HARBOR LIGHT 64
ELDRED ROCK LIGHT 176
Eldred Rock Lighthouse Preservation Association 176
Elliott Bay 167
Erwin, Walter 238

F
Fairpoint Harbor West Breakwater Light 22
Fathom Five National Marine ParK 222
FIRE ISLAND LIGHT 66
Fire Island Preservation Society 67
FISGARD LIGHT 224
Ford Madox Ford 121
Fort Jefferson 130
Fort William and Mary 89
Fraser, Charles 134
Fresne, Augustin Jean 11
Fresnel lens 11, 26, 28, 43, 47, 48, 55, 89, 91, 93, 94, 118, 122, 126, 138, 144, 152, 156, 168, 170, 176, 222, 252

G
GARDEN KEY LIGHT 130
GEORGES ISLAND LIGHT 227
Georgian Bay 222
Gibbons, Francis 200
Gibraltar Point 228
GIBRALTAR POINT LIGHT 228
Gig Point 222
Golden Gate National Recreation Area 164, 194
Grafton, Thomas 238
Grand Haven Pier Lights 25
Grand Haven River 25
Grand Manan islands 248
Grand Traverse Light 26
GRAYS HARBOR LIGHT 179
Great Duck Island 36
Grosse Point Light 28
Gulf of St. Lawrence 235

H
Hald, Andrew P.C 180
Halifax 237
Halifax Harbour Inner Range 227
HARBOUR TOWN LIGHT 134
Hamilton, Alexander 9
HECETA HEAD LIGHT 180
Heceta, Don Bruno de 180
Hefferan, Margaret 221
HENDRICKS HEAD LIGHT 68
Highland Light 60
Holland Harbor Light 30
Holland Harbor Lighthouse
Hillsboro Inlet 136
HILLSBORO INLET LIGHT 136
Hillsboro, Earl of 136
Hilton Head Island 134
Historical Commission 30
HOOPER ISLAND LIGHT 138
HUNTING ISLAND LIGHT 140
Huron, steam boat 30
Hurricane Camille 110
Hurricane Katrina 110
Hyannis Harbor Light 70

J
Jameson's Point. 90
Jefferson, President Thomas 60, 105
Jeffery, Captain John 168
Jones, William D. 216
Juniper Inlet 136
JUNIPER INLET LIGHT 142

K
Kennedy, Senator Edward M. 76
Keweenaw Peninsula 21
KEY WEST LIGHT 144
Key West Lighthouse Museum 144, 154
Kilauea Point 183
KILAUEA POINT LIGHT 183
Kincardine 240

L
Lady Elgin 28
Lake Erie 17
Lake Huron 36, 48, 222
Lake Michigan 18, 30
Leelanau State Park 26
Lee, Robert E. 143
Le Profound, ship 230
Lewis, Winslow 10, 78
Lighthouse Board 47, 100, 108, 172, 190, 194, 199
Lighthouse of Alexandria 10
Lincoln, President 36
Lincoln, President Abraham 110
LIME KILN LIGHT 184
Little Brewster Island, Massachusetts 8, 9
Liverpool Bay 250
Loggerhead Lighthouse *see Dry Tortugas Light* 128
Long Island Sound 94
Lord Ashburton, ship 248
LOUISBOURG LIGHT 230
Louisbourg Lighthouse Society 230

M
Mabrity, Barbara 144
Mabrity, Michael 144
Mackinac Island State Park Commission 39

Makapuu Point Light 12
Manitou Passage 26, 40
Mantiowoc Breakwater Light 32
Marblehead Coast Guard Station 17
Marblehead Light 34
Margaret's Bay 237
MARGARETSVILLE LIGHT 232
MARSHALL POINT LIGHT 72
Martha's Vineyard Historical Society 64
Matanzas River 156
Martus, Florence 121
Maugher Beach Light 227
Maurice river 62
Maury Island 202
McBeath, David 223
Meade, General George 11, 154
Meares, Captain John 172
Metcalfe, Brigadier General Orlando Poe 36
Michilimackinac State Park 39
Mississauga Point 228
Mississippi River 130
Moody, Dwight L. 246
Monomoy Islands, Massachussets 76
MONTAUK POINT LIGHT 74
Mount Desert Island 54
Mosquito Inlet 150
MUKILTEO LIGHT 187
Mukilteo Lighthouse Park 187

N
Nantucket Harbor 56
Nantucket Island 56
Nantucket Life Saving Museum 56
Nantucket Light (Great Point Light) 76
Narragansett Indians 102
National Historic Landmark 151
National Park Service 100, 121
National Register of Historic Places 56, 138, 188
Nauset Beach 78
NAUSET BEACH LIGHT 78
Nine Mile Point 228
NEW DUNGENESS LIGHT 188
Newfoundland Provincial Historic Museum 218
NEW PRESQUE ISLE LIGHT 36
New York Harbor 66, 100
NOBSKA POINT LIGHT 80, 81
NORTH CAPE LIGHT 235
North Carolina 124
Northumberland Strait 235

O
Ocracoke Inlet 148
OCRACOKE ISLAND LIGHT 148
Oglethorpe, James 161
OLD MACKINAC POINT LIGHT 39
OLD POINT LOMA LIGHT 190, 194
Olympic Mountain range 184
O'Neil, John 122
Oregon State Parks 174
Ottawa Point 48

P
Parks Canada 227, 235
Patapsco river 152
Patos Island Light 184
PEGGY'S COVE LIGHT 237
Pemaquid Point 83
PEMAQUID POINT LIGHT 82
Pigeon Point 192
PIGEON POINT LIGHT 192
Pinkham, Captain Paul 76
Poe, Colonel Orlando M. 11
Point Arena Tower 192
POINT ATKINSON LIGHT 238
POINT BETSIE LIGHT 40
POINT BONITA LIGHT 194
POINT CABRILLO LIGHT 196
Point Chehalis 179
POINT CLARK LIGHT 240
POINT FERMIN LIGHT 199
Point Loma Peninsula 196
POINT PINOS LIGHT 200
POINT PRIM LIGHT 243
POINT ROBINSON LIGHT 202
POINT VICENTE LIGHT 204
PONCE de LEON INLET LIGHT 150
Port Angeles 188
Port Townsend 188
PORTLAND BREAKWATER LIGHT 84
Portland Harbor 98
Portland Harbor Museum 98
PORTLAND HEAD LIGHT 86
PORTSMOUTH HARBOR LIGHT 88
Prospect Point Lighthouse 216
Puget Sound 187, 202

Q
Quick Sand Bay 172
Quoddy Narrows 105

R
Radelmüller, John Paul 228
Rawley Point Light 43
Ray, George 240
Rhode Island 102
ROCKLAND BREAKWATER LIGHT 90
ROSE BLANCHE LIGHT 244
Royal Canadian Navy 224

S
Saginaw Bay 48
Salter, Fanny May 13
Sandusky Bay 34
Sandusky Bay Light 34
San Francisco earthquake 164
SANDY HOOK LIGHT 10, 62, 96
Sandy Hook Lighthouse 62
Sankaty Head Golf Club 93
SANKATY HEAD LIGHT 93
San Pedro Bay 199
Savannah River 121, 161
SAYBROOK BREAKWATER LIGHT 94
Seabrook, Charles 143
SEAL ISLAND LIGHT 246
Seal Point 210
SEVEN FOOT KNOLL LIGHT 152
Seven Wonders of the Ancient World 8,10
Shaw, George 199
Shell Castle Island 148
Smith, James S. 210
Smith, John William 132
Smyrna Dunes Coast Guard 150
Snohomish Indian 187
SOMBRERO KEY LIGHT 154
South Carolina Maritime Museum 132
Spencer, Edward W. 28
SPRING POINT LEDGE LIGHT 98
Straits of Mackinac 36
St. Augustine 150
ST. AUGUSTINE LIGHT 156
St. Joseph North Pier Lights 44
St. Louis World's Fair 136
ST. MARKS LIGHT 159
St. Marks National Wildlife Refuge 159
Stanley Park 216
STATUE OF LIBERTY 100
Steam Navigation Company 243
Stevens, Isaac 187
Stevenson, Robert Lewis 12
Straits of Mackinac 39
Sturgeon Point Light 47, 48
Suislaw River 180
Susquehanna river 122
Swallowtail Keepers Society 248
SWALLOWTAIL LIGHT 248

T
Tawas Point Light 48
Thiersch, Hermann 8
Tillamook Bay 172
Thunder Bay Island 47
Trapier, Paul 132
Treaty of Point Elliott 187
Turkey Point Light 13
Turn Point Light 184
Twin River Point lighthouse 43
Tybee Island 121
TYBEE ISLAND LIGHT 161

U
U.S. Lighthouse Service 81
United States Lighthouse Establishment 62
US Coast Guard 22, 34, 41, 47, 52, 55, 64, 103, 108, 110, 126, 167, 172, 187, 192, 196

V
Vancouver Island 224
Vancouver Parks and Recreation Board 216
Vineyard Sound 80

W
Wadsworth, Henry 86
WATCH HILL LIGHT 102
Watch Hill Lighthouse Keepers Association 103
West Paseo Del Mar 199
WEST QUODDY HEAD LIGHT 105
West Vancouver Historical Society 238
WESTERN HEAD LIGHT 250
Wigwam Point 52
Wolcott, Rachel 34
WOOD ISLANDS RANGE LIGHTS 252
YAQUINA HEAD LIGHT 206
World's Fair 19, 43

Y
York River 58
Young, James 253
Young, John 240
Younghans, Maria 110

Acknowledgements

All images have been supplied under license by © Shutterstock.com.

The copyright holder credits the following images as follows:
Page 36: Phil Lowe, page 108, 110: Joseph Sohm, page 145: Fotoluminate LLC, page 152: Andrei Medvedev, page 162, 226-227 both: meunierd, page 198: Philip Pilosian, page 200-201 both: EQRoy, page 205: Sherry V. Smith, page 242-243, Karen Foley Phootography.

Page 210-211 Wiki Media Commons/Flickr/Dennis Jarvis

Bibliography

Wright Larry, and Patricia. *Great Lakes Lighthouses Bright Lights, Dark Nights*. Ontario: The Boston Mills Press, 1999.

Roberts, Bruce, and Ray Jones. *Eastern Great Lakes Lighthouses:* Ontario, Erie, and Huron (Second Edition). Quebec: Globe Pequot Press, 2001

DeWire, Elinor, and Paul Eric Johnson. *Lighthouses of the Mid-Atlantic Coast.* Stillwater: Voyageur Press 2002

Berger, Todd, and Daniel E. Dempster. *Lighthouses of the Great Lakes*. Stillwater: Voyageur Press 2002

Mitchell, Al. H*istoric American Lighthouses*. Bellevue: Barnes & Noble, Inc. 2003

Handy, Amy. American Landmarks *The Lighthouse*. Singapore: New Line Books Limited, 2006

Crompton, Samuel Willard and Michael J. Rhein. *The Ultimate Book of Lighthouses*. San Diego: Thunder Bay Press, 2001

Jackson, Sylke. *Lighthouses of North America Beacons from Coast to Coast*. Buffalo: Firefly Books 2013

Roberts, Bruce, and Ray Jones. *American Lighthouse*s. Old Saybrook: The Globe Pequot Press 1998

Roberts, Bruce, and Ray Jones. Southern Lighthouses Chesapeake Bay to the Gulf of Mexico. Chester: The Globe Pequot Press 1989

Grant, John, and Ray Jones. *Legendary Lighthouses*. Old Saybrook: The Globe Pequot Press 1998

Marcus, Jon, and Susan Cole Kelly. *Lighthouses of New England*. Stillwater: Voyager Press 2001

Roberts, Bruce, and Ray Jones. *Northern Lighthouses New Brunswick to the Jersey Shore*. Chester: The Globe Pequot Press 1990